THROUGH THE
SPANISH PYRENEES: GR11

ABOUT THE AUTHOR

If asked to describe my father, the word 'indomitable' invariably springs to mind. Dad's exploits formed a thread of marvellous adventure through our otherwise ordinary upbringing.

He first visited the Pyrenees more than thirty-five years ago and then a few years later, on honeymoon. The majestic and diverse mountains caught his imagination, but it was not until 1987 that he began to revisit them in earnest, first with the whole family, and later with interested friends. He undertook a number of solo trips collecting material *Through the Spanish Pyrenees – GR11*, published in 1996. For the second edition (2000), he walked the entire length of the trail in one expedition with his son. For this third edition, after more visits in 2003, he has revised the text and redrawn the maps and profiles. In 2000, for his Cicerone guide *The GR10 Trail*, he walked coast to coast again, this time on the French side of the range.

When not in the mountains, Dad, who lives in retirement in Shropshire, spends his time constructing a model railway (complete with Pyrenean castle, of course!), cycling and walking.

Dad always puts all of himself into his projects. I hope in reading this guide you will enjoy his company even half as much as I have, and still do.

Anna L Scamans

THROUGH THE SPANISH PYRENEES: GR11

A LONG DISTANCE FOOTPATH 'LA SENDA'

by
Paul Lucia

CICERONE

2 POLICE SQUARE, MILNTHORPE, CUMBRIA LA7 7PY
www.cicerone.co.uk

© 1996, 2000, 2004 Paul Lucia
Second Edition 2000
Third Edition 2004
ISBN 1 85284 404 3
A catalogue record for this book is available from the British Library.

ACKNOWLEDGEMENTS

I would like to thank my wife for her help in proof reading and for suffering my many absences whilst acquiring data for this guide. We still enjoy shorter walks together in the Lakes and Pyrenees. My thanks, too, to Rob and Dot Brammall, whose timely arrival at La Guingueta many years ago started me thinking about backpacking when illness had obliged me to give up running as a sporting pastime. Seeing a retired couple come into the campsite with heavy sacks, having walked quite some way along the GR11 in intense heat, made me think: 'If they can do that so can I'. Then there are my walking partners, Adrian Browne and my son Peter-John, who have spent many days and nights with me in all the weathers that mountains can provide, leaving us with memories of great times together and firing us with enthusiasm for yet more adventures ahead. P-J also accompanied me, during 1999, when we walked the whole route coast to coast in the regulation 44 days, earning ourselves a free beer at Chris Little's bar at Cabo de Creus.

Special thanks are due to Kev Reynolds for his enthusiastic encouragement at the start of this labour of love and for his advice and help along the way. I am also very grateful to those who have written to me, often with up-to-date information and observations on using the guide. Particular thanks to Michael Winterton, who has written to me at length of his adventures, imparting valuable facts incorporated in this revision. Finally, but by no means least, I would like to mention Jaume Vidal of Espot, who has always served me cheerfully, generously and kindly these past years. I still remember that he stored dehydrated and trail foods for me many years ago when he hardly knew me. His welcome was no less in 1999, greeting us with rum and cokes. My heartfelt thanks to all those who have made this guide possible.

Advice to Readers

Readers are advised that whilst every effort is taken by the author to ensure the accuracy of this guidebook, changes can occur which may affect the contents. A book of this nature, with detailed descriptions and detailed maps, is more prone to change than a general travel guide. New fences and stiles appear, waymarking alters, and there may be new buildings or eradication of old buildings. It is advisable to check locally on transport, accommodation, shops, etc, but even rights-of-way can be altered and paths eradicated by landslip, forest clearance and changes in land ownership. The publisher would welcome notes of any such changes for future editions.

Front cover: Ibón de Llena cantal and Balaitús (Day 13)

CONTENTS

MAP KEY

············	GR11
═══════	Motorway
─────	Busy main road
────	Minor road
─────	Pista
· · · · · ·	Path
─ ─ ─ ─	National border
──────	River or stream
····················	Railway line
	Lake

Contour heights are represented by shading starting at 300m and then at 500m intervals. NB. Each map starts with the lowest height band without shading.

⋏	Wild Campsite
▲	Campsite location
W	Water point
△	Trig. point
■	Notable building
†	Chapel
⸮	Daily start & finish

H/R/S/T/B/Re/C. Hotel/Restaurant/Shop/Telephone/Bank/Refuge/Camping site

Please refer to 'Sketch Maps' in the introduction.

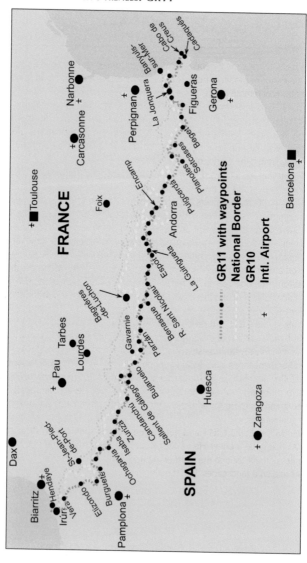

FOREWORD

In the past 30 years the Pyrenees have been 'discovered' – more than a century after a handful of pioneers from France, Spain and Britain made their sporadic explorations of remote peaks, passes and deep green valleys.

Thirty years ago mountaineering libraries in the UK contained only a few musty volumes devoted to this magical range. To learn about its history meant delving in obscure journals; deciding what to climb or where to trek during a proposed visit entailed poring over unsatisfactory maps and translating with schoolboy French the guides of Robert Oliver.

But all that has changed, and the number of English-language guides and travel books devoted to the Pyrenees is growing in response to a new wave of interest, partly from walkers and climbers weaned on British hills in search of something 'more exotic', and partly from activists tired of queuing at the foot of an alpine rock face. As a result of this explosion of interest some of the mystery of the range has gone, but not the magic. Whilst the few previously known centres have boomed in popularity, and certain barely known but accessible valleys have achieved a degree of status, there remain vast areas of true wilderness that see few visitors from one year to the next, and romantic, tarn-glistening glens where one could pitch a tent and live in seclusion for weeks of high summer listening to the silence.

Walking the GR11 will reveal some of those special places.

Paul Lucia, author of this guide, has been exploring the Pyrenees for many years and shares my enthusiasm for mountain, tarn and valley. This guide reflects that enthusiasm, and is a product of a number of visits to the Spanish flank, where he has followed this little-known but spectacular trail through regions of enchantment. To those who follow I would say: trek with your eyes wide open to the pristine grandeur to be found there, and ensure that it remains untarnished for future generations.

Few will walk the GR11 and not succumb to the spell cast by these mountains. As that great pioneer Henry Russell once wrote: 'It is to the Pyrenees that the smiles of the artist and the heart of the poet will always turn.' So, too, will the lover of fine wild landscapes. Join the club.

Kev Reynolds

El Cilindro (on the way to Monte Perdido from the Góriz hut) (Day 16)

PREFACE TO THE THIRD EDITION

The Pyrenees have become a very popular adventure playground. Roads now exist where only the pioneer once could stand. Even so, the GR11 is still a joy to walk, and I recall that I stood alone (or with my companion) on the last two mountains climbed along the route.

Some years ago there was a spate of new *pistas* cut to assist the farming community. Sometimes these tracks obliterated old GR11 paths, and there was a tendency to use these new routes even when old paths still existed. In 2003 I noticed that the tendency has been reversed, with some old paths once again being used for the GR11. *Pistas* cut in the mid- to late 1990s have sometimes caused older *pistas* to come into disuse, and these have effectively become footpaths. Please do bear this in mind, as even more route changes may be planned on the ground.

For this full-colour edition the maps and profiles have been redrawn and checks carried out throughout the length of the route. Two extra days are now used to walk this trail. The new refugio at Respomuso has become an obvious stopping point, and the route to it is waymarked on the northern side of the reservoir. The second day has been added because the new accommodation at Estaon is not always available and the only shelter is at Bordas de Nibrós. It is, therefore, a very long and hard day from Espot to the Bordas without a break, especially on a hot day, so a stopover at La Guingueta is the obvious choice.

I would like to thank Alan Castle, Robin Culverhouse, R. Glaister, Alan and Angela Greenwood, David Flannery and Jimmy O'Neill, Peter Flegg and Gill Yates, David Hanson, Martijn Molema, Kev Reynolds, Barry Smith, Wigger Uylenburg and Michael Winterton for taking the time to write to me with their observations and notes. These have been most useful in directing me in subsequent research.

Paul Lucia, 2004

DEDICATION

This edition is dedicated to the memory of Adrian Browne, a great companion in the exploration of the GR11 and other unforgettable Pyrenean adventures. He shared the summer snow in Val d'Incles, a violent, ear-shattering storm beside Ibons de Vilamorta, and many glorious and balmy days of high-level mountain walking. He is sadly missed, and both my son and I wish that we could have spent more time with him.

INTRODUCTION

The Spanish Pyrenees present a wonderland to the holidaymaker, whether backpacker, botanist, canoeist, cyclist, entomologist, mountain biker, skier, walker or simply anyone with a love of mountain scenery. Here, as an additional bonus, visitors can enjoy mountain landscape in a temperate climate. This guide addresses the needs of walkers on both day trips and longer expeditions. In recent years the mountain organisations and authorities in the administrative districts of Guipuzcoa, Navarra, Aragón, Andorra and Cataluña have got together with local villagers to arrange the waymarking of a coast-to-coast (Atlantic to Mediterranean) long-distance footpath designated the Gran Recorrido 11, GR11 for short or, affectionately, 'La Senda', to mirror the French counterpart GR10. This has opened up miles of waymarked footpaths and tracks in an ever-changing environment, often in remote and high areas, to numerous enthusiastic walkers of many nationalities, though the vastness swallows them up so that those seeking solitude will also not be disappointed.

ACCESS

The three main road routes from northern France towards the Pyrenees are Paris–Bordeaux, Paris–Toulouse and Paris–Perpignan. From these, roads reach the GR11. From west to east these are shown in the box on the following page.

French Rail, SNCF, run excellent services from Paris towards the Pyrenees. Three-day travel passes, valid for one month, include a return Channel crossing starting from Dover. However, planning the best route and being certain of connections requires specialist knowledge, and the travel agents supplying this service have gradually ceased to do so. It also takes some skill to work out how to get there and back on a three-day pass. Tickets for very fast TGV trains, as well as sleeping accommodation in sleepers or couchettes, are available with the payment of a supplement. For a little extra, Eurostar/SNCF combined tickets from London Waterloo can be obtained. Then it is possible to reach the Pyrenees from London within 12hrs, using Eurostar and the TGV.

To obtain the best discounts, the SNCF part of the ticket must be booked as a return from a specified zone and location. This is fine for one- or two-week holidays, when it is easy to return to the same station from where one started, but for end-to-end walking of the GR11 you are obliged to book to, say, Bordeaux or Toulouse and then to buy single tickets for the remaining journeys. Please note that it is best to book the return from Cerbère not Port Bou. There is only one through train a day from

Access Routes for the GR11

Bayonne – Irún	(day 1)	Lannemezan – St Lary Soulan – Bielsa Tunnel – Parzán	(day 19)
Bayonne – Irún – Vera de Bidasoa	(day 2)	Montrejeau – Viella – Viella Tunnel	(day 23)
Bayonne – Cambo les Bains – Puerto de Olsondo – Elizondo	(day 3)	Viella – Puerto de la Bonaigua – La Guingueta – Espot	(day 26)
Bayonne – St Etienne de Baigorry – le col d'Ispeguy – Elizondo	(day 3)	Foix – Andorra via Puerto d'Envalira – Arans	(day 32)
Bayonne – St Etienne de Baigorry – les Aldudes – P. de Urkiaga	(day 4)	Foix – Andorra via Puerto d'Envalira – Encamp	(day 33)
Bayonne – St Jean Pied du Port – Puerto de Ibañeta	(day 5)	Foix – Latour de Carol – Puigcerdà	(day 36)
Orthez – Port de Larrau – Ochagavia	(day 8)	Foix – Latour de Carol – Planoles	(day 37)
Oloron Ste Marie – Arette – le col de la Pierre St Martin – Isaba	(day 9)	Perpignan – Prats de Molló – Molló – Beget	(day 40)
Arette – le col de la St Pierre St Martin – Zuriza	(day 10)	Perpignan – Coustouges – Massenet de Cabrenys – La Vajol	(day 42)
Oloron Ste Marie – le col du Somport – Candanchú	(day 12)	Perpignan – Le Boulou – La Jonquera – La Vajol	(day 43)
Pau – Laruns – le col du Portalet – Sallent de Gállego	(day 13)	Perpignan – Banyuls sur Mer – El Port de la Selva	(day 46)
Lannemezan – St Lary Soulan – Bielsa Tunnel – Bielsa – Pineta	(day 18)		

Estany de Sant Mauici (Day 25)

View east from below Pic Superior de la Vaca (Day 38)

Port Bou but frequent ones to Cerbère, from where there are many departures northwards.

Bookings can be made at Rail Europe, who have a Travel Centre at 178 Piccadilly, London W1, tel: 08705 848848, **www.raileurope.co.uk**. I have found that acquiring a recent copy of Thomas Cook's 'European Timetable' together with the small local timetable slips from the railway stations, while visiting the Pyrenees, is most useful for planning rail access.

Below is a list of rail destinations with connecting SNCF bus services in italics. All connect with Paris. Only those of interest to GR11 walkers have been included. Taxis can be taken to the road head and thence by foot over the appropriate pass to the GR11 if there is no through road.

In addition to the above there is also a connecting service between Latour de Carol/Enveitg and

Rail Destinations and Linking Buses

Bayonne	–	Irún
Bayonne	–	St Jean Pied du Port
Pau	–	Oloron Ste Marie
	–	*le col du Somport*
	–	*Canfranc*
Pau	–	Oloron Ste Marie
	–	*Laruns*
Lourdes	–	*Cauterets*
Lourdes	–	*Gavarnie*
Toulouse	–	Luchon
Toulouse	–	l'Hospitalet
	–	*Andorra la Vella*
Toulouse	–	l'Hospitalet
	–	Latour de Carol/Enveitg
Perpignan	–	Banyuls sur Mer
		Portbou
	–	Llanca

Perpignan. The first part of this, in the upper Tet valley, consists of the 'Train Jaune', a narrow-gauge railway, which can be used to gain access by taxi then foot over high passes to Núria and Setcases.

One of the simplest ways to reach the Pyrenees is by overnight coach from London Victoria. However, the Eurostar/ SNCF combined ticket costs little extra and is much quicker. Coach travel is still a viable alternative for end-to-end walks. All coaches have onboard toilets, are non-smoking and have semi-reclining seats. A little care needs to be taken to reduce the discomfort of travelling 20hrs or so in cramped conditions. Take something to cover your eyes and something to stop your head rolling about. The coaches do stop for meals, but sufficient drinks and snacks need to be carried for the whole trip. Eurolines, tel: 08705 808080, **www.eurolines.co.uk,** run coaches to the following destinations:

- Bayonne
- Pau
- Lourdes
- Toulouse (connection for Andorra)
- Figueras
- Gerona
- Perpignan

The western section can be reached by ferry from Plymouth to Santander and then by coach to Irún. This is especially useful to those living in the West Country. Contact Brittany Ferries, **www.brittany-ferries.com.**

It is possible to obtain flights to Bayonne/Biarritz, Tarbes (Lourdes),

Toulouse, Pau, Perpignan, Gerona or Barcelona. These tend to be expensive unless part of a charter. No gas cans can be carried! However, RyanAir fly to Biarritz, Pau, Perpignan, Gerona and Barcelona offering very cheap fares. You can book online at **www.ryanair.com.**

GEOGRAPHY

The Pyrenean mountain chain can be said to have its beginnings as a rocky promontory on the Atlantic coast of Spain in the south-east corner of the Bay of Biscay and then to extend roughly east-south-east some 435km, as the crow flies, to another such headland on the north-west coast of the Mediterranean Sea. Any

Balaitous from Collado de Tebarray (Day 14)

Casamanyá from Coll de les Cases (Day 31)

walkers' route will almost double this distance.

From the western coast the range quickly rises to hills of Lake District proportions. Peña de Aia, at 806m, is but 12km in a straight line from Cabo Higuer. In the east, the rugged countryside is not quite so high. Roda, at 670m, is just under 3km from the coast at El Port de la Selva bay and just over 14km from Cabo de Creus. The range rises to over 3000m in the central part, with wooded ridges soon running down northwards to the farmlands of France, while waves of seemingly endless sierras sweep south into Spain arrested only by the Ebro river valley of Rioja fame.

An exception to this general picture is the delightful high mountain area of the Neouvielle National Park in France, north-east from the Ordesa. However, it is not surprising that the range's three highest summits are found on the Spanish side of the border. Monte Perdido at 3355m, Pico de Posets at 3375m and Pico de Aneto at 3404m therefore attract as much interest from those living north of the divide as from those in Spain.

Much of the central high ground and watershed is used as the international border between France and Spain. It will be noticed from maps that west of Andorra the high ground of the eastern section passes to the north of that coming from the west, thus forming the valley Vall d'Aran, which opens to the north-west into France. The two sections are joined at the eastern end of the valley by the high pass of Puerto de Bonaigua, used as a useful road to the south, complete with bus route.

Another interesting feature of note is that the meltwaters of the

17

small Aneto glacier pass underground at the collapsed cave called Forau de Aiguallut (Trou de Toro) and find their way underground, through the intervening ridge, to Vall d'Aran to join the River Garonne flowing into France. This passes through Toulouse and turns to the west to flow into the Bay of Biscay beyond Bordeaux.

The Pyrenees, being of a lower altitude and latitude than the Alps, do not have large areas of permanent snow and ice to limit the activities of walkers. More terrain in this range is therefore open to walkers as opposed to alpinists.

GR10 AND GR11 COMPARED

The two routes are similar in the Basque region. Navigation is difficult due to the plethora of trails compounded with the continual improvement and extension of *pistas* (rough vehicle tracks) for the farming community.

As mentioned in the 'Weather' section, below, the central and eastern parts of the GR11 become progressively drier the farther east one goes. The high and hot Spanish plateau to the south keeps wetter weather to the north at bay. In the high central area there is less forest, on the Spanish side, and therefore more exposure to the sun.

Both routes try to locate accommodation at the end of each stage. In France this is often achieved by using *gîtes d'étape* (private hostels). There is no equivalent in Spain, though recently it has become more common to find local homes offering overnight accommodation. These are known as *casas rurales*. Enquire at the local tourist office or bar.

There are a number of valleys on the Spanish side that run west–east

Estany Long (Day 25)

The author on Peña Ezcaurri, (Day 9)

and reduce the amount of ascent and descent required on the GR11. One dramatic difference between the two routes, therefore, is the fact that the total ascent along the GR11 is in excess of 39,000m, whereas the total ascent on the GR10 is over 49,000m!

EQUIPMENT

It is not necessary here to list in detail the equipment needed by mountain walkers undertaking this route as they will already be well acquainted with the lightest and best kit. Nevertheless, a few comments for those who would like some guidance may be useful.

First and foremost (and I cannot emphasise this too much) aim for the lightest load possible within the parameters of comfort and safety. There are two main differences between walking in, for example, the

English Lake District and the Pyrenees – the latter is much drier most of the time, with the exception of the lower western section; and you can spend more than one day walking up the same hill. This means that heavy loads are much more exhausting, especially if it is particularly hot, and that extra quantities of clothing are not required, as a daily wash will almost always be dry for the next use. A change of underwear, socks and T-shirt will be all that is necessary, though an extra set of underwear and socks will be useful on those rare occasions when washing does not dry.

Shorts are the preferred wear, though if trousers are worn they should be very light. Lightweight **boots** will be necessary and adequate, and **trainers** or sandals can be used over easier sections and road walking. Boots are not allowed in

19

Camping in the Coma Pedrosa (Day 31)

most of the manned mountain huts, and your own footwear is more comfortable than that which may be provided. As on all mountain walks, **waterproofs** must be carried.

The sun is particularly fierce on northern skins, so proper protection is needed for exposed parts. A **hat** is very useful, but make sure that light does not pass through it. I have suffered bad sunburn through a hat before I checked this!

Lightweight **stoves** are the order of the day for any cooking. If the preferred fuel is Camping Gas then canisters are fairly widely available. If re-sealable cans of Butane/Propane mix are used, then these can be purchased, to my knowledge, only in Benasque, south of the route, and in Andorra la Vella, also south of the route. However, there is a conversion unit available that allows Camping Gas cans to be used with Coleman-type stoves. Unleaded

petrol will have to be used for multi-fuel stoves.

A small sturdy **tent** will afford all the shelter, comfort and flexibility required. **Sleeping bags** really do require personal research. One has to juggle between weight and warmth, for those cold nights at altitude, and lightness, perhaps suffering the occasional cold night.

It is always advisable to carry at least some water in an easily accessible **water bottle**, and the text indicates when long distances have to be covered without any possibility of replenishment. Further lightweight water containers are essential in the drier areas. I take Platypus $2\frac{1}{2}$ litre containers, which can also be used with a drinking tube. Micropur MT5 tablets, obtainable from Boots, can be used to sterilise water.

Food will be according to personal preference, and again the text indicates if more than one day's supply is needed. Personally, I try to ensure that I have bread, condensed milk, coffee, some soups and maybe a little cheese as daily essential and emergency supplies.

Compass and **maps** should be carried, of course, the latter inside a waterproof case, just in case of rain (and the certainty of sweat!). Refer to the 'Map' section, below, for further information.

If you want to take photographs and don't expect to have them enlarged, then a compact **camera** perhaps with mini zoom would be ideal, especially now that very light models are on the market with even better lenses. For those who expect to have their masterpieces form large prints, either from slides or negatives, then a SLR or larger should be carried, perhaps with tripod, though this involves carrying extra weight. Digital cameras with quality lenses are now competing with film cameras in quality results. All this, plus individual bits and pieces, will need to fit into a strong rucksack, well tried out beforehand and adjusted for comfort.

MAPS

The Spanish 'Editorial Alpina' maps, complete with accompanying guide in Castilian Spanish or Catalan, used to cover only the central high mountain section, but now they have been improved and their scope extended to cover almost the whole route. These come in both 1:25,000 and 1:40,000 scales. Institut Cartogràfic de Catalunya produces fine maps at a scale of 1:50,000. The excellent French 'Randonnées Pyrénéennes' maps, at a scale of 1:50,000, have the path marked, sometimes incorrectly, but unfortunately often do not reach far enough south or have the very area required covered by the key, thus making them mostly only suitable for the GR10. The Castillian Spanish guide *GR11, Senderos de Gran Recorrido, Senda Pirenaica* (ISBN 84 87601 24 3), published by Edita Prames, contains a complete set of loose-leaf coloured maps at a scale of 1:50,000, complete with profiles. **Especially useful to GR11 trekkers is the new set of maps covering the whole route at a scale of 1:40,000**

Estany de Ratera (Day 25)

(ISBN 84 8321 062 2) also produced by Edita Prames. It is therefore no longer necessary to purchase the Castillian Spanish guide in order to obtain its maps, as these are available separately, though at a slightly reduced scale. Even so, there are still some glaring errors, and attention to the more important of these is given in the text. Please also note that it appears that many traditional way-point names have been omitted from this series, and other local or ancient names are sometimes used.

In the guide, at the beginning of the description of each day stage of the route, the relevant maps for that stage are identified. Accompanying the route description is a sketch map for each stage, showing the route in relation to the main geographical features. Notes on these appear under the section 'Sketch Maps', below. Walkers will also need to take the relevant map or maps for the sections walked, for map and compass work is still often required on these long-distance mountain trails, especially in the lower eastern and western sections.

Walkers should also ensure that they are familiar with the general geography of the area in relation to escape routes, both north and south, should these become required. Good road maps or the SGE 1:200,000 series maps are adequate for this. A photocopy of any relevant part would be adequate.

MOUNTAIN HUTS

These range in quality from hotel standard to bothies used as cow sheds. Information is given in the route description concerning usable places encountered on the route. Listed here are the main huts (refugios) along and close by the route, which have a guardian(s) resident during the period of opening shown. There is usually a small shelter alongside or near to the main

Refugio de Respumoso (Day 1)

building, though these tend to be closed when the main *refugio* is open (details in route description). Opening times are approximate, as these are dependent upon snow conditions and other variable factors each year.

There is no voluntary mountain rescue service in the Spanish Pyrenees similar to that in the UK. For any emergency assistance it will be necessary to first reach a telephone (mobile telephones sometimes will connect,

Mountain Huts

Casa Pablo (day 4)	Tel: (686) 41 96 15
El Aguila (day 11)	Open from June to October Tel: (974) 37 32 91
Valle de Aragon (day 11)	Tel: (974) 37 32 22
Respumoso (day 13)	Open all year Tel: (974) 49 02 03
Casa de Piedra (day 14)	Open all year Tel: (974) 48 75 71
Bujaruelo (day 15)	Closed in 1999 but may now have re-opened
Góriz (day 16)	Open all year Tel: (974) 34 12 01
Pineta (day 17)	Open all year Tel: (974) 50 12 03
Viadós (day 19)	Open end of June to beginning of October Tel: (974) 50 61 63
Estós (day 20)	Open all year Tel: (974) 55 14 83
Hospital de Viella (Refugi Sant Nicolau) (day 22)	Open all year Tel: (973) 69 70 52 (610) 97 72 64
La Restanca (day 23)	Open June to end of September Tel: (608) 03 65 59
Ventosa i Calvell (South of day 24)	Open 25th June to October Tel: (973) 29 70 90
Colomers (day 24)	Open mid June to October Tel: (973) 25 30 08
Amitges (day 25)	Open June to October, some spring weekends and possibly Christmas week Tel: (973) 25 01 09
Mallafré (day 25)	Open end of May to November Tel: (973) 25 01 18
Josep M Blanc (Variant, day 25)	Open June to September Tel: (973) 25 01 08
Colomina (Variant, day 25)	Open 15th June to 30th September Tel: (973) 25 20 00
Vall Ferrera (day 30)	Open from June to October Tel: (973) 62 43 78
Coma Pedrosa (day 31)	Open 21st August to end of October in first year of opening Tel: (376) 32 79 55
Estanys de la Pera (Variant, day 33)	Open July and August
Cap del Rec (Variant, day 33)	Open all year Tel: (973) 29 30 50
Ull de Ter (day 38)	Open June to end of September Tel: (938) 67 93 61

though not reliably) or guarded hut and, armed with a map with 'x marks the spot', contact the local Guardia Civil. However, finding a hut with radio or reaching a telephone can involve a long trek. Even though helicopters are now often used to evacuate the injured, rescue could still take some time. Therefore, great care must be taken to avoid injury or illness.

In these circumstances, and with the distances involved in some areas, a degree of personal commitment is needed over and above that required in British mountains. This actually adds to the sense of adventure and exploration, so that even in our modern times an element of personal resourcefulness and survival ability can be experienced. There are rescue service numbers appearing in Spanish guides, and those relevant are listed below. Bear in mind that mobile telephones do not always work in mountainous areas.

Mountain Rescue Numbers

Navarra Burguete	(948) 76 00 06
Roncal	(948) 89 32 48
Aragón Jaca	(974) 31 13 50
	(974) 36 13 50
Panticosa	(974) 48 70 06
Torla/Boltaña	(974) 50 20 83
	(974) 24 41 24
Benasque	(974) 55 10 08
Andorra	(9738) 21 2 22
Cataluña Camprodon	(972) 74 00 15

INSURANCE

Normal holiday insurance should be sufficient to cover basic holiday and medical needs. It is worthwhile shopping around. The demarcation between mountain walking and climbing is the use of a rope, in insurance terms. Most personal holiday insurance now covers hill walking,

Refuge de la Brèche (Excursion from Góriz) (Day 16)

Refugio de Tacheras perched on the ridge (Day 10)

rambling, scrambling and camping (i.e. activities that do not require the use of specialist equipment such as ropes and ice axes).

Take the original copy of the insurance with you to the Pyrenees, but leave a copy with a relative or friend at home. Also, check to see if emergency helicopter evacuation is covered. The form E111 should be obtained from the Post Office and presented to obtain free basic medical care in Europe.

TELEPHONE CODES

Most public telephones are connected to the international network. Calls from both France and Spain to the UK now use the same international code. Dial 0044 (then dial the UK number minus the first 0).

WAYMARKING AND NAVIGATION

The waymark signs are as follows.

*   White horizontal stripe above red on rocks, posts or trees means the correct route.
*   Red-and-white diagonal cross means incorrect route.
*   White horizontal stripe above red with added white directional arrow indicates change of direction.
*   Signposts are also marked red and white, labelled GR11, with direction and destination noted.

It is important to be aware that all marking over the whole 800-plus kilometres is done mainly by volunteers in their own time, so spare a thought for them when you have laboured up some interminable slope to great height to find comforting

25

Vallibierna junction (Day 21)

marks in very remote places. Please forgive them when you find yourself lost (misplaced) and wishing that the marks were more frequent.

Obviously time will erase any marking, and sometimes fresh undergrowth will hide old marks before remarking is carried out. Therefore skill in navigating through forests and mountain landscape will need to be re-enforced with the aid of compass and map. Locating the correct exit from places of habitation is particularly awkward. Help is given in the text. Also please note that:

- often, marking along *pistas* is infrequent
- there may not be marks in towns and villages
- marking is missing through most of the Sant Maurici part of the National Park of Aiguestortes and

Sant Maurici, except for occasional wooden posts
- there are no marks on the valley floor of the Ordesa National Park until the Circo de Soasa, though there are numerous other GR11-type marks beyond this
- in Andorra there are many GR11 variants differentiated by suffixes on signposts, though the route markings are identical and confusing.

In recent years there have been many changes taking place in the Spanish Pyrenees. New ski resorts, campsites and roads ever encroach upon the wilderness. Landowners, too, implement changes to the route of the GR11, frequently just after guides have been put to print! So do expect and prepare for some change to the data contained here.

One last, but by no means least, comment concerning navigation. The maps covering this route are not to the same standard as Ordnance Survey maps. Sometimes, when trying to triangulate a position, a mountain top will not be found to be in the exact place shown on the map, but extra points of reference solve the problem.

WEATHER

Generally it is much drier on the Spanish side of the divide, especially in the central and eastern sections, though the lower western section is subject to maritime winds and is much wetter on both sides of the border. By the end of May winter snow can clear sufficiently for safe progress to be made in the higher areas, but sometimes passes can still be blocked in mid-June, complete with threatening cornices. However, many snow slopes lasting into the summer can easily be surmounted without special equipment, once softened by the morning sun. Occasionally bitter winds can stop this process, and the steeper slopes cannot then be climbed without crampons, which would force a delay or use of an alternative route. It would therefore not be advisable to start a coast-to-coast walk, from the west, until about 7th June.

Frequently, while the GR10 in France is shrouded in morning cloud or mist, the GR11 is bathed in brilliant sunshine, thus warming early starts and urging walkers on to higher altitudes in order to assuage the heat of the day. The summer of 2003 was especially hot, and often the only way to cope is to start each day very early. This will often mean missing the breakfast provided, if using accommodation, and supplying this meal yourself.

Sunny days are very hot in the valleys, and storms do develop during the afternoon or evening on occasions, more so as the summer progresses.

A word of warning! The weather in mountainous areas can change rapidly from one extreme to another. Be prepared! Temperatures during storms can plummet to well below freezing, even in high summer, or raise the temperature to an uncomfortable high. The lowest summer temperature recorded on the top of

Pic de Ratera (Day 25)

The team, Bujaruelo (Day 15)

Aneto, the highest peak in the Pyrenean chain at 3404m, is minus 15°C. I have experienced, in early June, 33°C heat at 1300m, and a week later at 1700m endured a snow storm overnight. The previous day, in a bitter wind, standing water and stream edges were frozen at 2100m even during the sunshine from a cloudless sky. Overnight, four inches of ice had formed in the washbowl.

For the day walker, the possibility of weather change should hold no fears as a rapid retreat to the valley will save the day. For those undertaking longer journeys, suitable kit will be necessary for comfort and safety. Spring months of recent years have tended to be very wet and cold. The backpacker, snug in tent and sleeping bag, will have a warm and comfortable haven in all conditions. On the other hand, those walking the whole route from west to east will, no doubt, encounter very high temperatures during the final week.

WILD CAMPING

In addition to the comforts of proper campsites, the GR11 affords splendid opportunities for wilderness camping. An ideal camping site should have a clean water supply and a reasonably flat, clear, grassy area, as backpacking tent groundsheets tend to be fairly fragile. Of these places there are plenty. Walkers may find it useful to know the location of camping areas in advance – either for planning purposes or if, because of fatigue, threatening weather or for any other reason, a change of plans is required. Information on camping areas is therefore provided in this guide (see, for example, the Facilities Chart, below).

Usually it is not possible to camp above 2400m due to the boulder terrain, with the notable exception of an idyllic site beside Ibón de Llena Cantal overlooking the Balaitous Massif at 2450m on day 14; beside the waterfalls on the Punta de las Olas route on day 17 at about 2520m; and beside the lake below the Baiau hut, at about 2470m, on day 30. It is also difficult to find suitable spots when among the cultivated areas above villages. Camping is not permitted in national parks, though the Ordesa Park allows a bivouac, with or without tent, above 2100m at Soasa, and above 1800m in Añisclo,

though the tent should be removed by dawn. There are park rangers using 4x4 vehicles and binoculars to police the situation.

There is a general policy in northern Spain of no wild camping at all. In practice, backpackers camped in remote places away from roads or camped for survival reasons (exhaustion, injury or bad weather) are overlooked. The important thing, as always, is to be discreet and leave no evidence of passing. Rules with regard to camping at mountain huts vary. For example, at Goriz tents are allowed to be erected during the evening, but must be taken down during the day and left flat, if more than one night's stay is anticipated.

Camp at Esparvers (Day 33)

Collado de Tebarray (on the right), from Llena Cantal (Day 14)

WATER

Walkers must make their own decision about what degree of purity of water they feel is safe to drink. These notes are only a guide to assist in this choice.

Nearly all high mountain streams have good quality water, and I have not had any problems in drinking water from them. However, in the summer cattle are grazed at very high altitudes; therefore, during these months, all water from open sources should be sterilised. A map must be consulted before taking water to ascertain if there is any form of habitation upstream – bearing in mind that some refugios use the local stream as a drain/sewer! It is always good policy to take water from side-streams anyway.

Mountain lakes also can have good quality water, but more care is needed. Lower down, due to livestock and farmsteads, all sources should be treated with suspicion. Cheap bottled water from village stores can solve the problem of drinking water when there are no water points. Water points are noted both in the text and on the sketch maps in these lower areas.

WILDLIFE

Even non-botanists would find it hard not to be moved by the quantity and variety of flowers in the Pyrenees, often clothing whole mountainsides. Dog-tooth violets appear in the footsteps of the retreating snow. Elderflower orchids show soon after in their distinctive yellow or purple hues, at first glance looking like clumps of hyacinths. Most people are amazed at the quantity and variety of gentians. The large pendulous heads of the Pyrenean saxifrage decorating small crags also gain immediate attention.

Seeing the large birds of prey soaring overhead or sometimes below, when on the high ridges, is always exciting. It is possible to see several varieties of vultures. Griffon vultures, often confused with golden eagles at distance, are seen most frequently. Egyptian vultures are less often spotted, and there are rarer sightings of the bearded vulture or Lammergeier, distinguished by its large size and pointed wing tips. Red and black kites frequent lower altitudes. Both golden and Bonelli's eagles can also be identified. Carrying field guides while backpacking adds a lot of weight; I usually photograph flowers of interest and make field

drawings of any unidentified birds for identification at home.

NOTES ON USING THIS GUIDE

The route has been divided into numbered day stages. These stages are, of course, quite arbitrary, but have been devised so that, where possible, suitable places of accommodation are available at the end of each stage. However, shelter is not available at the end of all stages, and in such circumstances those without a tent will have to bivouac.

The route description for each day stage starts with a summary of the estimated distance, height gain and loss, and time required. The height figures have been rounded up as necessary. The times are, quite naturally, subjective, but are easier to attain than those shown in continental guides. They have been calculated,

Fire Salamander, seen around the Maladeta

and again checked on the ground in 1999, and are a suitable guide for fit persons able to maintain lengthy days of mountain walking carrying a load of 15–17 kilograms. During 1999, accompanied by my son and often with two other companions, we rarely took longer than the guide times, and I was the slowest. **The times given are the estimated walking time only**. Any time taken to pause or stop needs to be added. No account is taken for adverse weather conditions. Rain, mist, storms or exceptional heat will obviously affect one's performance. You should probably add another 20–30% to arrive at the total time needed from start to finish in fine weather.

More time than usual has been allowed for the uphill sections, bearing in mind that altitude and load often adversely affect those not acclimatised. (One advantage of the GR11 is that it often passes through villages where provisions and cheap meals can be obtained, which greatly reduces the weight of food that must be carried.) Walkers will soon ascertain whether they are going quicker or slower and will be able to adjust these times accordingly.

A profile is provided for each day with some waypoints indicated. Height scale is in metres and distance scale in kilometres.

Within each route description, the main locations along the route are given in bold. The figures immediately in front of the locations refer to the cumulative times in hours and minutes for the day. The figures following the location indicate its altitude, and are either the official map heights or estimated from the maps. In two places, the 'official'

Ibón de Cap de Llauset and Colladeta de Riu Bueno (Day 22)

heights have been adjusted, as these appear to be in error. On day 6 the Collado Superior de Morate seems to be about 1160m not 1060m, which I believe is the Collodo de Mozolo Artea height. The crossing of the Gave d'Aspe on day 11 is at 1560m not 1360m. Some place names are used from additional sources and will not be found on most other maps, but can be located on the sketch maps.

Place names used have not been translated (i.e. the text gives 'Collado de' instead of 'mountain pass of'), but a glossary of terms used in the guide and commonly found on maps has been provided in Appendix 1. Those unfamiliar with Spanish or Pyrenean terms will find a working knowledge most useful, and the glossary is intended to assist in this direction. The word 'road' in the text refers to a tarmac or concrete road only. For a stony or otherwise rough, unsurfaced vehicle track the continental word *pista* is used throughout. 'Path', 'track' or 'trail' denotes a footpath more or less distinct.

Compass directions given as N = north, ESE = east-south-east, etc, are to assist in choosing the correct route, especially where there appears to be a choice. Left and right, when in relation to a stream or valley, refer to the true left or right (i.e. when looking down the flow). The High Level Route (or Haute Randonnée Pyrénéenne) is referred to as HRP both in the text and on the sketch maps.

Tossal de Malo, Ordesa (Day 16)

SKETCH MAPS

There is a sketch map provided for each day. It is hoped that these will greatly reduce the walker's navigation problems. For this purpose, roads, *pistas* and paths are indicated by different symbols, with the GR11 route superimposed in red. While they are drawn to a smaller scale than other maps to the region, more route detail is shown. This can be most useful when negotiating the plethora of tracks in the western and eastern parts. Basic colour-coded contours have been included. Where other GR routes cross or pass along the same way, they are labelled for interest. Explanation of the symbols used is found in the map key.

METRIC CONVERSIONS				GR11 FACILITES LIST	

km	miles	m	ft		
0.5	0.3	100	328	H	Hotel or Lodgings
1.0	0.6	300	984	B/R	Bar/Restaurant
1.6	1.0	500	1640	S	Shop for victuals
2.0	1.2	1000	3281	C	Campsite
5.0	3.1	1500	4921	T	Telephone
8.0	5.0	2000	6562	Bk	Bank
		2500	8209	Re	Refuge with Guardian
		3000	9843	Hu	Unmanned Hut or Bothy
		3500	11483	Ca	Camping Area or Wildcamp

To convert to metric, multiply by the factor shown. For conversions from metric, divide by the factor.

In the facilities chart (opposite) the bold **Location** represents the terminus of the day noted in the left column. Items in *italics* are intermediate points with some sort of facility. An 'x' indicates that a facility is available. Water points are noted in the text and on the maps; consult the text for further infomation, as many of these points are totally dry at the height of summer. Note that unmanned huts are often used by shepherds who may lock them to protect their own kit.

Location	Alt.	H	B/R	S	C	T	Bk	Re	Hu	Ca
Cabo Higuer	42m		x			x				
Hondarrabia	5m	x	x	x	x	x				
Irún	5m	x	x	x	x		x			
Endara	240m		x							
Day 1 Vera de Bidasoa	56m	x	x	x	x	x	x			
Collado de Lizarrieta	441m		x							
Gorra	370m									x
Day 2 Elizondo	200m	x	x	x		x	x			
Day 3 Puerto de Urkiaga	912m	x								x
Casa Pablo	840m		x					x		
Day 4 Burguete	898m	x	x	x	x	x				
Roncevalles	952m	x	x			x		x		x
Day 5 Fábrica de Orbaiceta	840m						x			x
Day 6 Casas de Irati	860m									x
Day 7 Ochagavia	770m	x	x	x	x	x	x			
Day 8 Isaba	818m	x	x	x		x				
Day 9 Zuriza	1227m	x	x	x	x	x			x	
Day 10 La Mina	1250m								x	x
Ibón d'Estanes	2047m								x	
Day 11 Candanchú	1550m	x	x	x				x		
Camping Canfranc	1380m		x		x					
Ibones de Anayet	2227m				x				x	
Day 12 Sallent de Gállego	1305m	x	x	x	x	x				

Location	Alt.	H	B/R	S	C	T	Bk	Re	Hu	Ca
Day 13 Refugio de Respomuso	2200m							x		x
Ibón de Llena Cantal	2450m									x
Ibóns Azules	2400m									x
Day 14 Balneario de Panticosa	1640m	x	x					x		
Río Ara	2000m					x				x
Day 15 San Nicolás de Bujarulo	1338m		x		x			x		x
Puente de los Navarros	1060m				x					x
Ordesa restaurant	1300m		x							
Day 16 Refugio de Góriz	2160m	x						x		x
Añisclo	1800m									x
Day 17 Circo de Pineta	1290m	x	x			x		x		x
Plana Fonda	2100m									x
Day 18 Parzán	1144m	x		x		x			x	x
Central Eléctrica	1940m								x	x
Paso de los Caballos	2326m								x	
Es Plans	1550m				x				x	
Day 19 Refugio de Viadós	1740m							x		x
Plan d'Añes Cruces	2080m									x
Refugio d'Estós	1890m							x		
Santa Anna	1600m								x	
Day 20 Puente de San Jaime	1250m			x	x	x				
Benasque	1138m	x	x	x	x	x				
(3km south of route)										
Refugio de Quillón	1790m								x	

Location	Alt.	H	B/R	S	C	T	Bk	Re	Hu	Ca
Day 21 Refugio Puente de Coronas	1980m								x	
Ibón Inferior de Vallibierna	2440m									x
Ibón Superior de Vallibierna	2470m									x
Refugio d'Anglós	2220m									x
Day 22 Hospital de Viella	1630m					x		x		
Barranco de Rius	2340m									x
Day 23 Refugio de la Restanca	2010m							x		
Day 24 Refugio de Colomers	2115m							x		
Estany Obago	2236m									x
Refugio d'Amitges	2380m							x		
Sant Maurici	1900m							x	x	
Day 25 Espot	1320m	x	x	x	x	x				
Day 26 La Guingueta	945m	x	x	x	x	x				
Esterri d'Aneu	970m	x	x	x		x				
(4km north of route)										
Day 27 Bordas de Nibrós	1480m							x	x	x
Lleret	1400m	x								x
Day 28 Tavascan	1120m	x	x	x		x				
Boldís Sobirá	1480m									x
Day 29 Àreu	1225m	x	x	x	x	x				
Refugio Vall Ferrera	1940m						x			
(20 mins)										
Pla de Boet	1850m									x
Pla d'Arcalis	2000m									x

Location	Alt.	H	B/R	S	C	T	Bk	Re	Hu	Ca
Day 30 Refugio de Baiau	2517m									x
Coma Pedrosa	2250m								x	x
Arinsal	1466m	x	x					x		
Day 31 Arans	1360m	x	x	x						
La Cortinada	1350m	x	x	x						
(700m south of route)										
Ansalonga	1330m		x		x					
(2km south of route)										
Ordino	1300m	x	x	x		x				
(700m west of route)										
Day 32 Encamp	1280m	x	x	x	x	x	x			
Estany d'Engolasters	1616m		x							
Refugio de Fontverd	1880m								x	
Refugio del Riu	2230m								x	
dels Orris										
Refugio de l'Illa	2485m								x	
Day 33 Cabana dels Esparvers	2068m								x	x
Refugio Engorgs	2375m								x	x
Day 34 Refugio de Malniu	2138m							x		x
Refugio de Feixa	2160m								x	x
(private)										
Guils de cerdanya	1385m	x			x					
Saneja	1220m	x		x	x	x				

Location	Alt.	H	B/R	S	C	T	Bk	Re	Hu	Ca
Day 35 Puigcerdà	1204m	×	×	×	×	×	×			
Age	1160m	×	×	×						
Vilallovent	1170m		×							
Day 36 Planoles	1137m	×	×	×	×	×				
Torrente de la Extremera	1800m									×
Queralbs	1220m	×	×	×		×				
Day 37 Núria	1967m	×	×	×	×	×				
Refugio de Ull de ter	2200m							×		
Day 38 Setcases	1279m	×	×	×		×				
Molló	1184m	×	×	×		×				
Day 39 Beget	510m	×	×			×				×
Day 40 Sant Aniol d'Aguja	460m									
Refugio de Can Galan	800m								×	
Day 41 Albanyà	237m	×	×	×	×	×				
Molí d'en Robert	220m		×		×					
Massenet de Cabrenys	372m	×	×	×		×				
(10mins)										
Day 42 La Vajol	515m	×								×
La Jonquera	110m	×	×	×	×	×	×		×	
Day 43 Sant Quirze de Colera	165m		×							×
Llanca	15m	×	×	×	×	×	×			
Day 45 El Port de la Selva	12m	×	×	×	×	×				
Day 46 Cabo de Creus	15m	×	×							

The Maladeta range beyond the Estós valley (Day 20)

DAY 1
Cabo Higuer – Vera de Bidasoa

Distance:	30km (18.6 miles)
Height gain:	830m
Height loss:	815m
Time:	7hrs 15mins

For those who are fortunate enough to have six weeks or so available to walk the whole trail from the lighthouse at Cabo Higuer to Cabo de Creus, overlooking the Mediterranean, this must be an exciting time. And it is no less exciting for anyone fit enough to start the first part of this varied and entertaining walk. An adventure indeed! It is time to exercise mountain navigational skills or to develop them during these lower (by Pyrenean standards) early days through the Basque wooded hillsides. Even the passage through Irún can be borne in the knowledge that one will soon be in the countryside and lost to the frenetic world in which we live, even if for only a short while. Food for one day only will be

Maps: IGN Carte de randonnées Pays Basque Ouest. Editorial Alpina Bidasoa Belate (from Collado de Erlatz). Prames maps (1:40,000 and 1:50,000) 1. Prames maps still show the route climbing to the Ermita de San Marcial, but waymarks follow sketch map route.

Profile Day 1

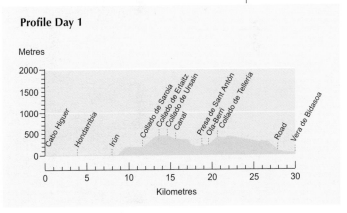

required if it is intended to reach the town at the end of this stage.

Please note that the Endara lake is not shown on some maps! Please also note that the route has changed from that shown on the IGN map and previous guides. If arriving by air at Biarritz, it is best to take a taxi to Biarritz railway station and then a taxi from Irún station to either the youth hostel, Albergue Juan Sebastian Elcano, C. Faro, or the campsite, Jaiz Kibel, C. Guadalupe. **Note:** The Hostal at Vera, at the end of the first day, can often be full, so ring 948 630 392 to reserve a room.

0.00 Cabo Higuer, 42m. From the lighthouse go

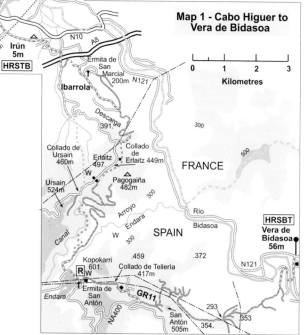

Cabo Higuer

down the road, S, taking the first left down the road with the No Entry sign, through the zigzags towards the fishing port, turning right to follow the coast road SSW then S to Hondarribia. *The mountain seen ahead is Peña de Aia.* Here the road turns from the coast SW to pass the airport leading to the bridge carrying the main N1 road. Pass under the bridge to a large roundabout. The GR11 once turned left here to follow the north side of the main road, without a footpath, but now goes across the roundabout and up the road, Calle Fuenterrabia, SE to the bridge over the main railway line, where it curves left, ESE, to pass through the centre of Irún by the main street.

1.20 Irún, 5m. *A large border town geared to tourism. Extensive construction (2003) at the lower end of the town may make it difficult to find the way. Make for the low ground eastwards to the Arroyo Errotasarko and Ibarrola road.* Pass through the town ESE taking the Paseo de Colón and the Avenida de Navarra to join the road beside the stream going south to Ibarrola. This means following the street Paseo de Colón until it turns slightly left and starts to go downhill. Continue E, pass a stream beneath the road and then take the first street that slants away ESE to the right. In a few metres go across a staggered crossroads, and you should now see a paved pathway to the left of some flats. Follow this path to the road, bearing left, E, over a stream, by a small bridge, to join the Ibarrola road. Turn right, S. *Both GR121 (Old GR11 route) and GR11 markers seem to be missing in 2003.* Shortly, pass beneath the A8 motorway and just

Camping: Campsite Faro de Higuer, just west of the lighthouse, no longer accepts tents. The two bar/restaurants are still open. There is another site, Camping Jaizkibel, 2km west of Hondarrabia. A youth hostel at the northern end of Hondarrabia is recommended. There are no other suitable places to camp during this day, with the possible exception of just below the dam of San Anton beside the pista, where there is a small stream coming off the hillside to the west, although this is a very public place.

Cabo Higuer

before the high-tension wires turn left, E, taking a steep stony *pista* that goes in a long curve left then right to pass beneath the power lines before climbing E with a long section of steps to the left of the track. At a farm the way becomes concrete, leading to the road junction above. *The route no longer goes via the Ermita de San Marcial.* Turn right along the road and take the concrete road on the right at the first bend, which goes steeply down at first and leads to a small pass. Bear right, taking the *pista* that goes up S, curving around the eastern slopes of Descarga, soon climbing parallel to some power lines to the left. Then after a bend with a stream, the *pista* passes under the power lines to a farm gate and cattle grid. Go through the gate and take the concrete road to the right that climbs first eastwards then westwards to the power lines again. *There is an old path from before the gate that climbs steeply beneath the power lines to this spot, but it is very overgrown.* Just before the cables, turn left, S, up the hillside over grass. Take the right fork, S, by a white building to the road coming up from Ibarrola passing between the two summits of Erlaitz, 497m, and Pagogaña, 482m, at the...

3.35 Collado de Erlaitz, 449m. Continue WSW, parallel to the road on its SE side passing a spring (dry in 2003). The track becomes vague and passes over a small grassy lump to...

3.50 Coll d'Ursain, 460m. There are black-and-yellow-painted posts on each side of the road. *Another such post farther along the road indicates the route of the*

GR121 going down. About 7mins down this track is a good water point with an emergency camping possibility on the left a few minutes before it. Beside these posts, take the descending *pista* SW, on the E side of the road, soon ignoring the path going straight on. *The mountain ahead is Peña de Aia, much closer now.* The *pista* descends in huge zigzags. Turn right, WSW, at the next junction, and at the next sharp bend where the *pista* turns SE avoiding a deep valley, on the right, over a low fence, probably hidden by bushes, is found a narrow watercourse and tunnel. *This is the canal carrying water from the Endara lake to Irún. The GR11 follows the concrete edge of the canal for 20–30mins, and some-times the sheer drop to the left, though not large, can be unnerving. It is also very narrow. Those suffering from vertigo should consider continuing down the* pista, *which also leads to the San Antón dam.* Go along the canal edge, against the flow, and after passing a build-ing, about 20mins later, look out for an iron gate on the left with a signpost above on the right. *Here one passes from Guipuzcoa into Navarra.* Go through the gate and follow the path steeply down SE through trees to a small stream. Turn left to join the *pista* and turn right, SW. *There is the possibility of an emergency camp along this* pista *by a stream coming from the right.* The *pista* becomes a road climbing steeply up to the dam.

5.00 Endara (Presa de San Antón), 240m. Turn left across the dam and follow the road to the turning to the bar/restaurant Ola-Berri. Take the road up to the bar with the chapel of San Antón below and have a nice break. Water can be obtained from a hose if the bar is closed. From the west side of the bar take the rough farm track that goes up beside it and climbs E between fields and power lines to reach the…

5.20 Collado de Tellería, 417m. Go down E past the Tellería farm on the left to a cement road, which climbs to join another. Turn right, SE, and climb up the cement road, which bears left overlooking open fields and other isolated buildings. At the top of the road, as it turns right, carry straight on into the wood along a *pista*, ESE. In about 500m turn left, at a GR11 No Way mark, and then immediately right. This *pista* climbs gently to a fork. Bear left and follow the *pista* down N, going under two power lines, and then take the next gravel *pista* on the right that turns SE around the summit of San Antón. Bear left at the next fork and go down through a zigzag, avoiding vague turnings to the left. At a clear junction, turn right, climbing easily through the wood. Follow the *pista* to the left of the white building, ESE, contouring the grassy point 354, then going down beneath power lines to a junction…

6.30 a small coll at 293m. Please refer to the sketch map. Do not continue along the *pista* seen ahead, NE. Find the waymarked old *pista* just to the left, also ascending NE at first, beside a fence; not the one on the far left. Avoid turnings right and left. The *pista* narrows to a track before joining the main *pista* about 20mins later. Go down left to the road. The road goes down to the river. Turn right at the cross-roads and then S to the first old narrow bridge over the river, which is crossed, and a left then a right turn along a narrow lane leads to the main road. Turn left for the Hostal Euskalduna at the next main turning to the right, which is the main street of the rather spread out town of…

7.15 Vera de Bidasoa, 56m. *Hotels, restaurants, shops bank, telephone, bus service to Irún and to the south. Most services can be found about 600m east. There is also a* casa rurales *near to the Hostal.*

Risco de San Antón (Kopokarri) 601m

DAY 2
Vera de Bidasoa – Elizondo

Distance:	30km (18.6 miles)
Height gain:	1130m
Height loss:	985m
Time:	7hrs 15mins

Today the route leaves the Rio Bidasoa and continues in a south-easterly direction gaining high ground and many passes, three of which contain small road crossings, the first at the very border. Then it turns south past the Collado de Iñaberri to the Río Baztan and Elizondo. This is a long day of woodland trails, open ridges and strange and enchanting place names.

0.00 Vera de Bidasoa, 56m. Turn eastwards along the main road beside the *hostal*. About 350m later, at a small roundabout, turn right at an open square, S, to climb a gravel-covered *pista*, ignoring another climbing to the right, passing the swimming pools seen to the left. Just above the pools the *pista* is joined from the right by the

Maps: IGN Carte de randonnées Pays Basque Ouest. Editorial Alpina Bidasoa Belate and Alduides Baztan. Prames maps (1:40,000 and 1:50,000) 2. Please note that the Prames 1:40,000 map indicates wrong exit from Vera. The route is also incorrectly marked on the Prames Spanish Guide 1:50,000 map as it leaves Vera.

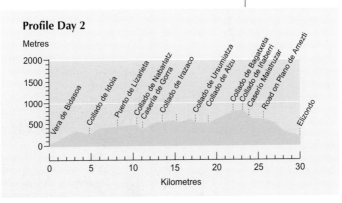

Profile Day 2

Metres

Vera de Bidasoa · Collado de Idoia · Puerto de Lizarieta · Collado de Nabarlatz · Casería de Gorra · Collado de Irazaco · Collado de Ursumiatza · Collado de Aizu · Collado de Bagatxeta · Caserío de Iñaberri · Caserío Maistruzar · Road on Plano de Arnezti · Elizondo

Kilometres

Camping: There is a suitable place south of the farm Gorra.

other road that climbs from the south side of Hostal Euskalduna. Follow the road upward, S, to the farm called Migelteneko-borda. *Water point.* Go up a stony path SE, which becomes grassy and is joined by a farm *pista* on the left. Go up the *pista* and look out for a sharp turn left, NW,

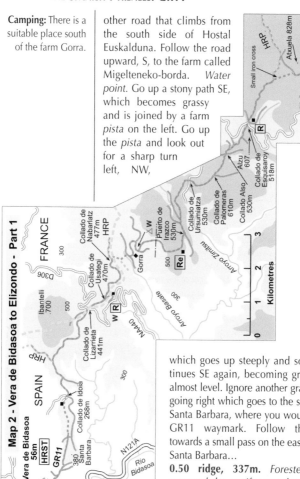

Map 2 - Vera de Bidasoa to Elizondo - Part 1

which goes up steeply and soon continues SE again, becoming grassy and almost level. Ignore another grassy *pista* going right which goes to the summit of Santa Barbara, where you would find a GR11 waymark. Follow the *pista* towards a small pass on the east ridge of Santa Barbara…

0.50 ridge, 337m. *Foresters have removed the conifer wood on the hill ahead. It is possible to turn right going steeply down the pista to join with another that winds and climbs to the next pass.* However, follow the *pista*, E, through the debris of the old plantation, aiming to meet the fence line just to the right of the small hill, point 366, where a gate allows access into the fields beyond. Cross the fields by gate and stile to a gate to the right of the farm, Larrete-Enea, where a grassy track then concrete road go down to…

1.15 Collado de Idoia, 268m. *The narrow road going back to the left, NW, goes to Vera.* Go up the *pista*, with Ibantelli ahead, past white farm buildings to a signpost marking the junction with the High-Level Route. Turn right, SE, and climb this *pista* easily around the SW and E faces of Ibantelli to reach the frontier with road crossing and bar/restaurant at…

2.05 Collado de Lizarrieta, 441m. Frontier marker No.44 in the vicinity. Cross the road and follow a large *pista* that goes up SE beside the border on the French side, passing a path to the right going down to another bar/restaurant, Usategi, to reach the Collado de Usategi or Palomeras, 470m, frontier marker No.46. The *pista* continues to marker No.50 and…

2.30 Collado de Nabarlatz, 477m. *New water point on left beside cabin at about 470m reported. The High Level Route continues along the* pista. The GR11 turns SSW

Vera de Bidasoa

going down a path over grass, and shortly leaves this path to turn sharp left, SE, going down to the Basate stream. Cross the stream, turn right and then left at the next fork, climbing S to the farm...

2.50 Casería Gorra, 370m. Go up the *pista*, SE, which turns to the right to join another coming from the left, signpost. Turn sharp right, NW, following this *pista* round to the south again. Shortly, take a left branch SE, which passes by a *water point* and possible spot for the tent. Follow this *pista* as it makes a sweeping curve around Centinela over the pass of Cerro, 550m, past a new unnamed *refugio* to join a *pista* from the right continuing ENE to...

3.40 Collado de Irazco, 530m. Shortly the High-Level Route takes the left branch while the GR11 takes the right branch, continuing ENE and ignoring another branch shortly going off to the left. Go along the left of the ridge, ENE, with the Solaberriko-Turria valley on the left and the Zimizu to the right until a...

3.50 Highpoint, 570m. The *pista* turns SE crossing the ridge and goes down to the...

3.55 Collado de Ursumiatza, 530m. Cross the little road and go up the *pista* S then SE to...

Santa Barbara ridge with Peña de Aia still in view

4.10 Collado Palomeras, 610m. Go down SE, passing the Collado Also, 530m, where the *pista* on the left of the ridge ahead is taken, SE, contouring the NE side of Alzu. This leads down to another road crossing at…

4.35 Collado de Esquisaroy, 518m. *The* pista *going down right goes to the bar/restaurant Esquisaroy.* Cross the road and climb steeply SE by an old deeply eroded *pista*. The gradient eases as the trail wanders SE above the Esquisaroy valley to a fork by a small iron cross on a wooden post (the post may now have rotted away) where the High-Level Route bears left along the *pista* while the GR11 bears right up a path to the right of the ridge. It then goes down to join a *pista* coming from the left. Continue southwards along this *pista*, more or less level, passing the small pass of…

5.20 Collado de Bagacheta, 793m. Follow *pista* SSW to…

5.35 Collado de Iñaberri, 795m. *The pass between La Ronda to the NE and Urrizpil to the SW.* Continue along the *pista,* which goes down southwards through a beech wood, with Urrizpil on the right, to a clearing. Take the left fork of the grassy *pista* to a zigzag; not many waymarks from now on. Then go S and SSW to reach a building with a spring nearby called the Fuente de Maistruzar. Go down by the *pista*, SSE, which is rutted and scattered with boulders, with the upper Arla stream to the left. About 15mins later take the turning to the right which goes up SW a short distance before turning left to meet the new road at a picnic area…

6.15 Plano de Amezti, 580m. *The road here goes along to the hill of the same name and then down by zigzags to Elizondo. The GR11 takes short-cuts across the loops down the obvious south ridge.* Turn left and continue down along the road to the small hill ahead called Amezti, 627m. Just before the road rises to the top of the hill beside a white house, bear left across rough ground to find a track going southwards, below and to the left of the house, down to the road again. If the track is overgrown, or there is shooting heard, just follow the road to the next section. Turn left; go around the bend to

Map 2 - Part 2

Irrizpil 800 · ·850 La Ronda
Collado de Iñaberri 795m
W · Maistruzar
Regatta de Arla
Plano de Amezti 580m
500
· Amezti
300
HRB ST
TV Elizondo 202m

Caserío de Maistruzar

a short-cut going off left once more, with the town seen below. The track goes down to and across the road to a *pista*, through the wood to a wooden gate. Turn left SE along the *pista*, becoming a road going past the telephone relay station, then the school and clinic of Nuestra Senora del Pilar, to the SW end of main road through...

7.15 Elizondo, 202m. *Hotels, bars, restaurants, bank and shops. Information office opens only in the summer. Non-resealable gas cans available at the Ferreria. Turn left just before the river to find accommodation, with use of kitchen, at Casería Salias with restaurant opposite.*

DAY 3
Elizondo – Puerto de Urkiaga

Distance:	18.5km (11.5 miles)
Height gain:	1050m
Height loss:	340m
Time:	5hrs 35mins

Today, for the first time, the route tops 1000m. Walk the border ridge for a kilometre, enjoying beech woods and grassy ridges. As always, care must be taken with navigation, and mist will make it easy to become disorientated. However, the 7km of high ridge from the border to Collado de Enekorri has a fence to guide the way. Some slopes could be slippery in rain. There are no lodgings available for this stage, so a camp or bivouac will be necessary around the final pass. Two days' provisions are required.

0.00 Elizondo, 202m. Leave the town by the Avenida Monsenor Mauricio Berecochea, SSE, on the SW side of

Maps: Editorial Alpina Alduides Baztan. Prames maps (1:40,000 and 1:50,000) 3. Prames maps show the descent to Urkiaga down a pista to the north of the old route, but this is a path. The pista follows a different course. See sketch map!

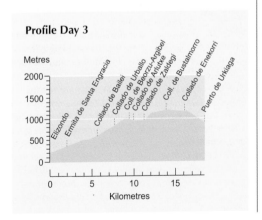

Profile Day 3

53

Map 3 - Elizondo to Puerto de Urkiaga

Elizondo 202m
HRST
Ermita de Santa Engracia 354m
Borda Venta
.521
500
697.
300
500
Collado de Bailei 606m
Larrebeltzeko 962m
Collado de Urballo 890m
GR11
Peña de Alba 1074m
Collado de Beorzu-Argibel 960m
Collado de Arlutxe 936m
FRANCE
SPAIN
Collado de Zaldegi 947m
Argintzo 1213m
Peña de los Generales 1165m
GR12
Collado de Bustalmorro 1180m
Collado de Zagua 1170m
N138
Puerto de Urkiaga 912m
Collado de Enekorri 1140m
1000

0   1   2   3
Kilometres

the large church. Go up the road for about 500m, where it turns to make a large curve to the left. Go straight on, signpost pointing the way, until the road is met again which is followed to…

0.35 Ermita de San Engracia, 354m. Here it becomes a *pista* climbing towards the SSE. Within 1km it turns towards the south, then makes a sharp right zigzag to gain height just before the farm, Borda Venta, over on the right. Continue along the *pista*, SSE then S, to…

1.35 Collado de Bailei, 606m. *Water point on the left.* Here the *pista* turns SE. Avoid the turn to the right going SW but go straight on, SE, soon taking the left fork. This goes up the left side of the ridge ahead a short distance before crossing to the right side to continue climbing SE, passing another water point, then E to…

2.30 Collado de Urballo, 890m. *Situated between Peña de Alba to the SE and Larrebeltzeko to the NW. Hunters' cabin to the right with spring.* Here the *pista* ends. Go straight ahead over the grass ESE to just before a fence where the trail turns right, S, passes through some trees, and climbs to…

2.50 1000m contour. *Camping possible, with water from a small stream. This was in thick cloud the first time that I passed this way and I got accidentally shot at. The shot passed harmlessly over my head and I continued, singing loudly.* Follow the frontier ridge and fence S to, first,

Collado de Beorzu-Argibel, 960m, then along the narrow part of the frontier ridge to Collado de Arlutxe, 936m. The frontier turns to the left but the GR11 continues down, S, avoiding a number of tracks descending SSW. The trail joins a rough *pista* coming from the right, which goes to...

3.35 Collado de Zaldegi, 947m. *Hunters' cabin to the right with stone tables and benches.* The GR11 goes up to the higher of the two huts above, turning north for a short while before turning left to gain, above the rough ground, the north flank of Peña de Los Generales, 1165m. Climb SW up steep grass and turn south to cross the fence coming down from the summit at its lowest point. Continue SSW contouring Argintzo, 1213m, over on the right, to join the fence again at...

4.25 Collado de Bustalmorro, 1180m. *The GR12 joins here from the right.* Continue S, contouring the eastern side of Arsal, 1259m, to the next pass, Collado de Zagua, 1170m. Continue S over the grass, the shooting hides on the left and fence on the right, towards the little hill ahead. The fence on the right begins to turn towards the east. Then look out for a gate in it with hunters' cabin amongst the trees on the other side. This is...

4.50 Collado de Enekorri, 1140m. *The route no longer goes down the* pista *on the other side of the fence.* From the gate, an ENE bearing leads to a post marker, and on the other side of the grassy rise a rough path descends ESE. This is well marked and passes various locked huts and shooting hides to join with a *pista*. Turn left to the pass seen a short distance below...

5.35 Puerto de Urkiaga, 912m. *Chains usually at the entrances of the pistas. Notice-board with footpath map. Water behind nearby hut on eastern side of the road. The flow was poor in July 2003 and the obvious area for a tent can be fouled. However, a tent can be erected on top of the bunker seen above and to the left of the track. Otherwise, it would be necessary to continue to the water point beyond the gate or Casa Pablo. About 7km to the north the road passes into France. For bunker shelter, try up the* pista, *not the shortcut to the left.*

Camping: Wild camping by the Puerto de Urkiaga with water at the locked cabin, or use a suitable wartime bunker up the pista of next day's stage. There is also the possibility of a camp just over the Urballo pass. There is also a water supply beside a locked hut just beyond and below the metal gate above Puerto de Urkiaga, about halfway to Collado de Adatun, where another possibility exists.

DAY 4
Puerto de Urkiaga – Burguete

Maps: Editorial Alpina Alduides Baztan. Prames maps (1:40,000 and 1:50,000) 4. There is a short-cut across the long bend of the *pista* climbing from Urkiaga and an earlier route down to Barranco Odia. Neither is shown on the Prames maps.

Camping: At Barranco Odia or around Casa Pablo. There is a campsite 2km south of Burguete.

Distance:	16km (9.9 miles)
Height gain:	680m
Height loss:	695m
Time:	5hrs

This is another day of grassy high ridges, fence lines and beech woods. Care with navigation is required, and again mist would make this much more difficult. Rain will make some slopes slippery.

0.00 Puerto de Urkiaga, 912m. Take the stony *pista* E, which climbs through the wood, with many bunkers offering refuge in bad weather. A short-cut across the first long bend of this *pista* has been waymarked, but this misses some of the bunkers. About 25mins later take the left fork of the *pista* and, a few minutes later, a path on the right, S, which ends at a metal gate. Go through the gate and follow the track to the SE. *Slightly to the left is a short section of pista and then grass down to a locked hut with external water supply.* The trail contours around the north face of Adi, 1458m, turning towards the east, through a patch of trees to... **1.05 Collado de Adatun, 1213m.** *A large grassy area.* The crag ahead is passed on its north side. Go down a little across the grass, E, to locate a large and clear waymark indicating the start of the ascending traverse of the rocky slope through the

Profile Day 4

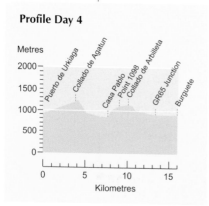

wood. Take great care in the wet, as this rock is very slippery and precipitous in places. The waymarks lead upward, with the ground becoming easier, out of the wood and up to the fence line. *The route no longer goes up to the west ridge of Iturrumburru (called Collado de Iturrumburru), 1300m. It may still be the best way in wet conditions. In which case, continue to the fence coming down from the left, cross the one on the right and go SE down the slope to the Barranco Odia.* Cross the way-marked stile on the right and go

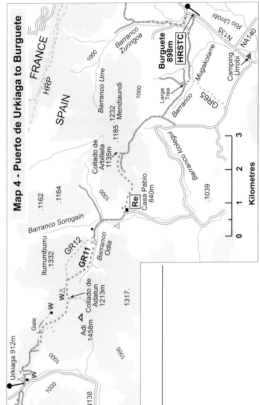

steeply down through the wood – very slippery in the wet. The way is clear after about 10m, going down to the Barranco Odia. Turn E along a grassy *pista* to cross the Sorogain stream to the new *pista*. Turn right, S, and follow this *pista* to...

2.15 Casa Pablo, 840m. *A road going south starts here.* **Casa Pablo has been extended and now offers full refugio services.** *It is possible to camp nearby.* From the north of the building, take the path eastwards, over a stile, going up to the ridge ahead. The waymarks are followed ESE steeply to the ridge and fence above. Turn left at the fence, NE, to continue climbing steeply to point 1098m, where the gradient eases. Follow the fence upward. Soon, clear waymarks on a fence post are seen. It is possible to cross here and follow the track parallel with the fence, but it is better to continue easily upwards, with the fence on the right, NE then W to...

3.15 Collado de Arbilleta, 1135m. The fence continues to Mendiaundi, but the GR11 crosses it by a stile here to go down a grassy track SSE and, in a couple of minutes, cross another fence to a *pista,* which is followed SE steeply down through the beech woods. This is covered with sand after the sand quarry. About 2km later, at a metal gate, this is joined from the right by a newer *pista,* which is followed SE. In just over 1km the *pista* turns left to a tree, with large change of direction marks, at the corner of a wood with open farmland ahead. Turn right and follow the edge of the field to the right. At the last corner the St James of Compostela route, GR65, with yellow markers, joins from the south through a gap in the hedge. Turn left along the edge of the field, where the track widens, passes into a wood and crosses two small streams to gain a narrow passing place giving access to a large *pista* that eventually goes past farm buildings (left), then a footbridge over the Barranco Suringoa. The steep stony road leads to the main road through...

5.00 Burguete, 898m. *Turn right for hostal/restaurants. Turn left for supermarket just down left from the main road at the next junction with telephone booth opposite. Hotels, bars, restaurants and shops. The road going north reaches the border with France then on to St-Jean-Pied-du-Port. Go 2km south to Camping Urrobi that sells butane non-sealable gas cans.* **Note:** *Fresh bread arrives at the panadaría only after 11am. Accommodation, youth hostel and meals can also be found at Roncevalles.*

DAY 5
Burguete – Fábrica de Orbaiceta

Distance:	20.5km (12.7 miles)
Height gain:	600m
Height loss:	660m
Time:	5hrs

Maps: Editorial Alpina Roncesvalles. Prames maps (1:40,000 and 1:50,000) 5.

Camping: Along the river north of Fábrica de Orbaiceta. The best place is on a grassy shelf above the *pista* beside the barranco Txangoa. There is also an unguarded campsite at Arrazola beyond the Fábrica.

From Burguete the trail passes through farmland then woods to Roncesvalles, with its large abbey – founded as a stop-over for pilgrims on their way to Santiago and still used for this today. The trail continues on to Puerto de Ibañeta, often in cloud, before climbing to the high ground of Astobiskar, turning south down a *pista* to the old munitions factory Fábrica de Orbaiceta. The high area tends to be wet with low cloud, so care will be needed with navigation. Provisions for three days are required.

0.00 Burguete, 898m. Take the road WNW down past the supermarket crossing the Barranco Suringua. Ignore

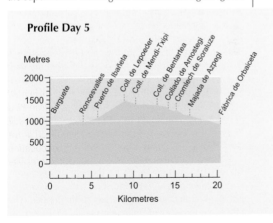

Profile Day 5

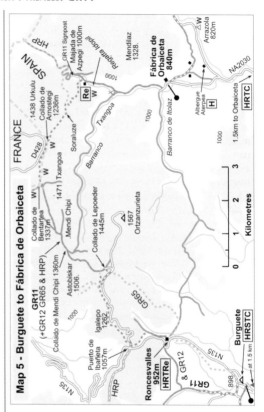

Map 5 - Burguete to Fábrica de Orbaiceta

a *pista* to the right. About 300m from the town, at an open grassy place, turn right, N. Ignore GR11 marking ahead, which would take you left around farm buildings to yesterday's stage, but go N. Avoid taking either the road or the *pista*s on the left, and cross a small stream by a narrow footbridge and continue N along the road. About 20mins from town, go through an iron gate, continuing along a *pista,* and soon take a grassy *pista* NE, gaining access through a gap in the barbed wire fence into the wood. Continue generally NE passing an open area and junction. The *pista* joins a cement road coming from farm buildings on the right, which climbs a short way to the N, then turns E to meet the main road at a sharp bend. Turn right, down to...

0.55 Roncesvalles, 952m. *Accommodation, including youth hostel, pilgrim hostel, meals and tourist office. An important monastery on the pilgrim route.* **Please note that a Pilgrim Credential Card is needed to gain access to the pilgrim hostel. This can be obtained from the monastery pilgrim room.** Turn right at the tourist office; pass along walkway and down steps. Turn left through an arch to the northern courtyard containing the youth hostel. Pass through another arch; turn right down to the GR11 *pista* and turn left. Follow the *pista* N, taking a wide trail on the left, sign-posted 'Ibañeta', to...

1.20 Puerto de Ibañeta, 1057m. *Here there is a monument to Roland and a GR11 signpost. The HRP joins from the W. The Lepoeder pass can be reached by walking up the narrow road going E. It can be avoided by following the GR11, a harder climb NE along the ridge.* Take the narrow road E for a few minutes until the first large curve to the right, where waymarks indicate a narrow track on the left climbing NE. The trail passes Igalepo off to the left, arriving at a grassy pass near the road. Take to the road here and climb easily to a short-cut on the left, which climbs to...

2.20 Collado de Lepoeder, 1445m. *The GR65 coming from Roncesvalles joins from the S at the short-cut and so, all friends together, the GR11, GR12, GR65 and HRP unite for a while. The summit of Astobiskar, 1506m, can be reached to the N in about 20mins, but steps have to be retraced to join the GR again, though it is possible in clear weather to come down the steep NE ridge to the Collado de Mendi Chipi.* Take the *pista* that goes down N and then turns NE to contour the SE side of Astobiskar to reach, on the NE ridge...

2.40 Collado de Mendi Chipi, 1360m. *The* pista *going down sharply to the right also goes to the destination for the day and is a very pleasant walk.* The GR11 crosses to the northern side of the ridge and continues ENE along a

61

Roncevalles and Burguete

relatively level *pista* of Roman origin, avoiding a *pista* going up right and another going down to the left as the route passes below the summit of Mendi Chipi and Txangoa. At a junction about 150m after leaving the wood with a ladder stile over a fence ahead, the Compostela trail turns left while the GR11 takes the right fork for a few metres before turning off left, E, to cross the fence by another ladder stile just S of the first one. This is the...

3.05 Collado de Bentartea, 1337m. *Frontier between France and Spain, border stone No.200. Water point, 200m down Compostela trail. The next water point was not working in 2003. Follow the frontier E then ESE by a vague grassy pista with the fence line to the right. Look out for border stone No.201, for below, S, is an important water point – easily seen and ideal for a lunch break. Continue along the N side of the fence, though one can use the water point side, to the marker stone 205 and...*

3.35 Collado de Arnostegi, 1236m. *Over on the left, on the summit of Urkulu, are the remains of a Roman watchtower, possibly with an earlier ancestry. The road to the left comes from St-Jean-Pied-du-Port, which makes* *this pass popular, especially at weekends.* Leave the frontier ESE by a clear track above the steeper slope. Just over 1km later the track passes to the left of some large stones identified by a sign as the Cromlech of Soraluze. The track goes down E and very shortly takes a track on the right *(the HRP continues straight on here)*. The GR11 no longer crosses the stream below, as the route now follows the yellow marks from Soraluze. At a Cromlech signpost go S over grass, passing a small stream. The path turns E then SE to join with the *pista*, just below...

4.10 Majada de Azpegi, 1000m. *The GR12 goes N.* Follow the main *pista* S, passing a *refugio* with water supply both inside and out. *The* pista *from Collado de Mendi Chipi joins from the right in just under 2km.* Look out for camping spots if it is intended to camp, as there are no suitable places after the Fábrica until the ruins of Arrazola.

5.00 Fábrica de Orbaiceta, 840m. *A group of buildings next to the old armaments factory. There is a bar, the Ostatu Urkulu, which appears to be permanently closed. Accommodation and a meal may be had at the village of Orbaiceta, 4.7km south by road. Where the GR meets the road on the next stage, there is a camping area with water at Arraozla, a deserted hamlet some 500m down this road. Another 1200m down the road is Albergue Aterpea, which opens only in July and August.*

Maps: Editorial
Alpina Roncesvalles.
Prames maps
(1:40,000 and
1:50,000) 6.

Distance:	16.5km (10.3 miles)
Height gain:	400m
Height loss:	380m
Time:	4hrs 15mins

A much easier day, allowing a detour to the summit of Mendi-Zar for a panoramic view. The route climbs the Regata de Arrazola to the southern flank of Mendi-Zar before descending the Morate valley to touch the border, then continues south to the large man-made lake of Irabia. The *pista* then leads to the camping area at the end of the stage.

0.00 Fábrica de Orbaiceta, 840m. Ascend the cement road, E, beside the bar. In about 10mins or so take the left fork to a farm where the trail continues as a *pista*, E, along the right side of the Regata de Arrazola, gradually turning to the NE. After about 20mins, take the right

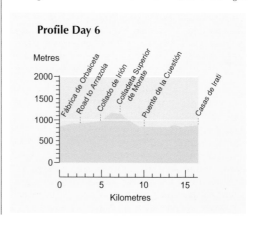

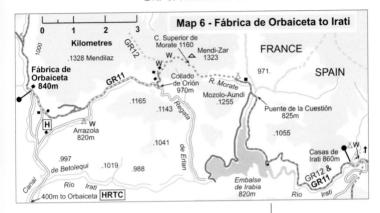

Map 6 - Fábrica de Orbaiceta to Irati

fork *(the main* pista *continues to a forest pista that descends back to the GR11 pista)* to the road from Arrazola, some 500m to the south. Turn left and after 2km the road turns ESE, then with a left and right turn it arrives at the…

1.10 Collado de Orión, 970m. Take the *pista* that goes steeply up N. It is reported that the route is now well waymarked. Just below the second building on the left, take a track on the right, which goes down past a cabin and water point. From here ascend the track NE which joins with the GR12 again as it comes from the left. Another water point is reached at the head of the Regata de Erlan, where it may be possible to find sufficient level grass to camp. Continue ENE towards the summit of Mendi-Zar as a guide, keeping above the treeline to the right. There are several tracks contouring the south of Mendi-Zar. Keep to the one nearest the treeline. *The upper one reaches the ridge ahead at some rocks with clear waymarks, but these lead nowhere. The entry point for the descent through the wood is about 100m below, in the distance. If in cloud and the rocks are located, either go steeply down the ridge, or go steeply down through the wood using the first small valley to the E of the ridge until the GR is located.* The track gradually turns SE to contour the south flank of Mendi-Zar before

Camping: Available at the head of the Regata de Erlan, the lower part of Regata Morate and Casas de Irati. Other possibilities indicated on the map. The camping area shown on the Spanish Guide map at the head of the Arrazola stream has a No Camping sign, and any water in the stream is likely to be polluted due to cattle grazing here.

65

crossing the grassy ridge with two isolated and faintly waymarked trees at…

2.20 Colladeta Superior de Morate, 1160m. *From here a steep climb to the top of Mendi-Zar can be made in about 30mins, returning by the same route.* Go down E into the wood. Look out for the waymark on a tree indicating the entrance point. Go down steeply through the wood, watching out as the GR turns NE just before the streams. Cross a stream and follow the path down SE, about 10–15m above the Morate stream seen on the right. This leads to a grassy *pista*, which passes a hut to the left, suitable for overnight shelter, and many places to camp. Follow the *pista* to cross the Morate stream turning right, S, to reach…

2.55 Puente de La Cuestión, 825m. Cross the bridge turning S along the *pista* beside the lake, Embalse de Irabia. Much later, avoid a turning to the right going down to a private cabin, but turn left, NE. Climb the *pista* leading to various loops and bends, which take you to the Río Irati, which then is followed eastwards along its right bank to a bridge that crosses the river to join the road end from Ochagavia below the ruins of…

4.15 Casas de Irati, 860m. *A camping spot can be found by crossing the bridge and taking the path to the chapel, but turning off right below the Casas and then down a farm track, ENE, to a small meadow with water supply.*

DAY 7
Casas de Irati – Ochagavia

Distance:	14.5km (9.0 miles)
Height gain:	670m
Height loss:	760m
Time:	4hrs 20mins

Maps: Editorial Alpina Roncesvalles. Prames maps (1:40,000 and 1:50,000) 7. Prames maps do not show new route from Irati.

This stage goes generally southwards, through the lovely and extensive forest of Irati, crossing the Abodi ridge, with splendid views in every direction. There are lodgings and provisions available at the end of the day. The GR11 has been re-routed a number of times to avoid the 5km road climb from the Casas de Irati to the ridge that gives access to Abodi. Navigation could be tricky in cloud, especially finding the route off the side of the Abodi ridge. **Note:** There is no certainty of any water today until Muskilda, so sufficient water must be carried. A new ascent route has been waymarked and this is described here, though the old route, just after the 19km road marker, is still waymarked.

0.00 Casas de Irati, 860m. From the bridge go up the road, E, which curves round to the W. Thirty metres before the notice-board at the first bend and opposite the *pista* going down left, turn right, SSW up an earth bank and cross grass to a sign post. A few minutes later fork right to the road. Cross the road and take the path opposite, taking the right fork, SSW, some 20m later. Soon join with a *pista* going SSW. This soon comes to the road again, where a track is

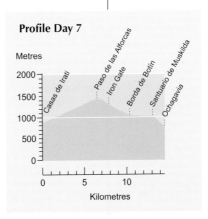

Profile Day 7

Camping: Camping Osate, 500m south of Ochagavia on the eastern side of the river. It's best to cross the bridge over the Río Anduña to the main square. Exit the square by opposite corner to locate new road (lower one of the two) passing by new buildings to the camp. 5mins slow walk. Open all year (except Nov).

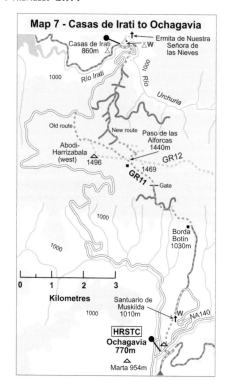

Map 7 - Casas de Irati to Ochagavia

followed WSW beside it. Bear left and climb *pista* SSW, ignoring a left branch. Much later, a forest track is crossed, continuing SSW up a *pista* slightly to the right. A few minutes later the direction changes to SSE before crossing the main forest *pista* shown on most maps. Continue SSW on the other side. After a few minutes, take a left fork SSE, then another SSW and yet another SSE along a grassy track. About 10mins later fork left, S, along a path and then fork right, SE, up a path. A few minutes later, at another fork, turn right, ESE, to the open hillside. *In cloud, care is needed to locate the pass.* Go SW up steep grass to post marker and marks on rocks.

Then go SSE to signpost. SSW leads to the pass in a couple of minutes. *Please note that the pass lies to the east and beyond a large sinkhole.*

2.15 Paso de las Alforcas, 1440m. *The GR12 continues E from here.* Go down S over grass by a vague path to a shepherds' hut with two rooms in good condition. From the hut go E at first, keeping above the steeper ground, then SE above the woods. About 10–15mins from the pass look out for an iron gate in the fence below, and turn S down a grassy ridge to reach it. Go though the gate and follow the grassy *pista* S to a clear *pista* turning E. Shortly follow waymarks across grass to the right, down to the stream. Climb back to the *pista* above and at the gate continue straight on, with gate and fence on the left, to the second stream. Cross this and follow the rocky path S then SE through bushes to the edge of the wood and…

3.10 Borda Botín, 1030m. Take the *pista* SSE along the ridge turning S to join the road coming up from the left and Ochagavia. Turn right and follow the road SSW to…

3.50 Santuario de Muskilda, 1010m. *Water point and picnic area.* Pass through the sanctuary or pass by on the right if the gate is locked, and on the other side go down the steep steps and old cobbled path, SSW, all the way to the cobbled streets of Ochagavia. Bear left down through these to reach the centre of…

4.20 Ochagavia, 770m. *Hotels, restaurants, lodgings, shops, bank and campsite selling non-sealable gas cans.*

DAY 8
Ochagavia – Isaba

Maps: Editorial Alpina Roncesvalles. Prames maps (1:40,000 and 1:50,000) 8.

Camping: There are no suitable camping spots due to the lack of water.

Distance:	23.8km (14.8 miles)
Height gain:	710m
Height loss:	660m
Time:	5hrs 35mins

An unusual day in that one could go all the way to Isaba on the *pistas*, though the GR11 descends through the woods by a different route. It is also a dry day, so water will need to be carried, especially as there is no shade above the forests. There is a hut for shelter about half way, but no water. The *pista* climbs gently through the woods east of Ochagavia to follow wide ridges and pass around the north face of Kakueta before taking a complex but well-marked route down to Isaba.

0.00 Ochagavia, 770m. From the main square go to the River Anduña and take the cobbled street NE on the south side of the river to a building showing an

Profile Day 8

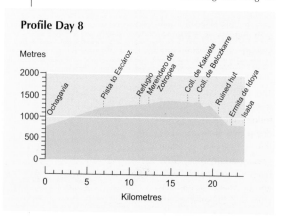

'Exposition' sign. Pass between it and another showing 'Estación de Patatas'. Follow the road right then left, which becomes a *pista* ascending NE. This climbs and turns back above the town before turning E. *It is easy to locate one's position along this long route by the direction of travel and reference to the sketch map as the route changes direction quite distinctly from time to time.*

1.50 Junction with pista to Nebazkene and Ezcároz, 1210m. Continue SE. Some time later avoid a *pista* to the right but take the one turning NE. Much later the *pista* makes a loop to the north, passing a hut to the head of a valley. There is also a hut here, but no water. Then it heads SE to...

2.45 Merendero de Zotrapea, 1300m. *A picnic area with and junction with the GR13.* Ahead, SE, one can either take the *pista* or go over the grassy hill. Both rejoin to pass to the right of Lakuaga Sierra, 1415m, near to a signpost, continuing along the ridge to the north face of Kakueta, which is contoured to finally climb NE to...

3.45 Collado de Kakueta, 1365m. *Here the* pista *turns sharp right, S, to contour the E of Kakueta.* The GR11 has been re-routed. Turn left, N, and follow the earthy *pista* down to a sharp bend to the left above a small grassy saddle seen close below. Look to the right, and waymarks and a clear path will be seen gently ascending the side of the

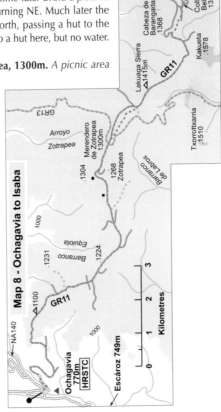

Ochagavia

hill over grass. This joins another earthy *pista*. Continue E taking the right branch in a few metres, which climbs a short way to...

4.00 Collado de Belozkarre, 1370m. Look out for the marks directing you to go down yet another earth *pista* to the right, and almost immediately turn left down a path through the trees following the marks E down to the earth *pista* a short distance below. This *pista* is now overgrown and only a narrow, clear path remains. Go E down the *pista* for about 5mins, and where the bank on the left comes down to the level of the *pista*, take the clear path, sharp left at a No Way mark, NW. **Note:** *It is possible to follow the pista-cum-path all the way to Isaba. Only the last short section is steep and covered with loose rocks.* The trail curves around the head of a small wooded valley, crossing two streams, before heading ESE again. Then it goes down a ridge through thorn bushes. Take care to take the right branch (though the left branch is no longer clear). This goes to a ruined building, where another sharp left is taken NNW, through more thorn bushes, to find the path and way-marks leading down and turning E, following a fence line seen to the left. Take care to locate the waymarks on this steep descent. They keep to the left of the more obvious routes down through the trees as they lead to a change of direction marker on a tree indicating a right turn, S. This takes place some way above the valley, with the buildings seen down below through the trees. Go S along this ancient sunken track for several minutes before turning left, E, to go down a few metres to pick up another path going S. The first building you come across is the…

5.20 Ermita de Nuestra Señora de Idoya, 825m. *16th-century chapel with attending vicarage and spring nearby.* Pass through the hermitage to find on the other side a cobbled track going S to…

5.35 Isaba, 818m. *Hotels, bars, restaurants, shops, bank and HI hostel. Climbing the main road through the village, the panadaría is first seen up on the left, with the tourist office down to the right. A little further on, there is a sign to the youth hostel, Albergue Oxanea, up some steps to the left. B&B can be obtained opposite the hostel. The road climbs and turns left to the top of the town, where a supermercado can be located on the left. Beyond the supermercado and further down left is Hotel Ezkaurre, with reasonable restaurant.*

Maps: Editorial
Alpina Ansó. The
GR11 route is
incorrectly marked
to the summit of
Peña Ezcaurri.
Prames maps
(1:40,000 and
1:50,000) 9. Prames
maps do not show
the alternative
waymarked route
along the Belabarze
valley.

Distance:	18.5km (11.5 miles)
Height gain:	1300m
Height loss:	890m
Time:	6hrs 30mins

Today's stage is a superb mountain expedition in its own right, taken as a one-day hike. But, as part of a continuous long-distance walk, it is extremely arduous, with 300m of crag to surmount after hauling loads up some 1000m to the foot of the south face of Peña Ezcaurri. One cannot believe that walkers are expected to surmount this obstacle, but the gully cannot be seen until right up against the rock, as it starts diagonally left behind the first pillars. Keenness to scramble is needed here; it is not at all difficult, though awkward to start, and it has two awkward rock steps to surmount. So a decision

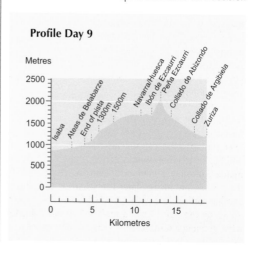

Profile Day 9

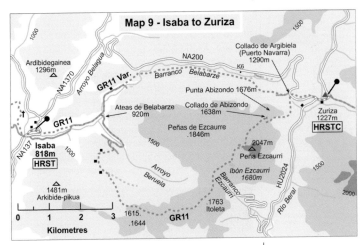

Map 9 - Isaba to Zuriza

has to be made to avoid this stage by the northern route if it is too intimidating. Water will have to be carried, as after the early river there is none.

0.00 Isaba, 818m. From the telephone boxes in the town centre on the main road, cross what looks like a bridge, E, and go up the Calle Barrikata to soon reach an old path passing by the small hermitage of Belén. The path joins a *pista* coming up from the lower part of town. Follow the *pista* E to the junction of the two valleys called…

0.35 Ateas de Belabarze, 920m. Turn right across the bridge, S then SE. *If you have decided to give this part a miss, then follow the instructions in the box below.* In just over 1km the *pista* crosses the stream, becomes earth and begins to climb steeply NW. Go up this for a few minutes, passing an earth *pista* climbing very steeply to the left. A few metres later turn sharp left, S, along another earth *pista* with waymarks present and a fence above on the right. Keep a look out on the right, for when the fence turns sharply upward, you must leave the *pista* (waymarks) to find a path beside the fence

Camping: At Zuriza with bar and restaurant. The water is foul at Ibón d'Ezcaurri in high summer.

ascending WSW. When the fence makes another sharp turn to the right, ignore old marks on posts and continue upwards, W, on grass up to a ruined hut. *Beware of biting flies in the open grassy areas.* Continue W to a wide track and then S over grass to another ruined hut. Go SE from here on another wide path following waymarks to a third ruined building. Continue upwards, passing to the right of some rocky outcrops. Continue SE up the ridge to reach a grassy place overlooking a valley to the north-east. There are a number of tracks ahead contouring the mountainside and some waymarks, but all arrive well below the pass beyond Itoleta. The true

Espelunga, on the Alano ridge, seen from Collado de Abizondo

route continues to climb SE before gaining the top of the ridge, with its grassy summits. Then it turns E to gain the SW ridge of Itoleta to contour NE, level with the pass ahead. The path passes above the treeline to reach the border between Navarra and Aragòn at the pass above the Barranco Ezcaurri…

3.15 Pass, 1740m. Continue N, passing rocky outcrops on the E side, climbing slightly, and avoiding a clear path that goes left around the last rise and would take you to the pass between Peñas de Ezcaurre and Peña Ezcaurri. Continue down NE to the western side of the most westerly glacial lake of the Pyrenees…

3.40 Ibón d'Ezcaurri, 1680m. *Please note that the Spanish Guide map shows the route passing to the wrong side of the lake. The only escape from here involves a long descent SE then S to the Barranco de Ezcaurri and a 5km road walk up to Zuriza. It is not possible to go through the pass on the left and find an easy and safe way down without first climbing back to the summit plateau.* Follow the marks to the south face of the mountain. A short steep section gains access to the ascent gully. There are two more steep steps, awkward but not difficult, before you come out on the summit plateau. Follow waymarks NE to the summit platform…

5.00 Peña Ezcaurri, 2047m. Leave the summit slightly west of N to pick up the obvious marked descent route on the north flank, which takes an easy fault line down the northern slabs. This goes down to the clear pass…

5.40 Collado Abizondo, 1640m. Go down NE through the dense stunted beech wood, turning back to the mountain for a while before continuing down NE. The steepest section will be very slippery in wet conditions. The waymarks lead down to the road a few metres below the…

6.10 Collado Argibiela, 1290m. Turning one's back to Navarra, cross the road and follow the path down, E, to join the road again in about 1km. Follow the road to the campsite with its entrance above and on the north side…

6.30 Zuriza, 1227m. *Excellent campsite, open all year, with helpful staff. Hotel, bar, restaurant, shop and*

*Peña Ezcaurri from
Zuriza*

*dormitories with a free hut nearby – keys at the bar. Out
of season, when the shop is closed, staff will bring in
supplies from Ansó upon request.*

Belabarze route

From the Ateas, take the *pista* NE to its end.
However, do not cross the stream but take the path
that climbs ahead. Once in open ground, turn right
at a post marker, cross the stream by small footbridge, seen behind bushes to the left, and then an
E bearing will lead to a tree with waymark that can
be hidden by tents when school parties are camping
here. The waymarked path stays close to the stream,
except to pass obstacles, and is easy to lose, but
continue E on the south side of the stream. Much
later, it is important to spot the right fork changing
direction to SE. This occurs opposite a distinctive
crag on the opposite side of the valley and just
before the end of a fenced arable field on the left.
The trail climbs indistinctly over grass through trees
before becoming clearer, turning ESE to join with a
pista. Turn left, E, and the pass is seen ahead. The
other route joins the road a short distance below
and is marked with a cairn. This part should only
take about 3hrs.

DAY 10
Zuriza – La Mina

Distance:	12km (7.5 miles)
Height gain:	735m
Height loss:	740m
Time:	4hrs 05mins

Maps: Editorial Alpina Ansó. Prames maps (1:40,000 and 1:50,000) 10. Marked route at La Mina not correctly shown on Prames maps.

They said, at the campsite, that this was a lovely walk and it proved to be so. Towering limestone crags overlook the start, and no major difficulties make for a relaxing day, with the certainty of a good meal in the evening.

0.00 Zuriza, 1227m. Take the *pista*, SE, on the right-hand bank of the Barranco Petraficha, passing a new water point after 15mins. About 2.5km from Zuriza, as the *pista* goes across the stream, take the path steeply ascending E past the…

0.50 Refugio de Tacheras, 1410m. *Usually in good condition.* Continue climbing NE above the hut, eventually passing above a grassy area with a metal shepherd's hut below to the right (the Refugio de Chipeta Alto). Continue the ascent, E, with the trail following a rocky ridge in the centre of the valley. As usual, the first pass seen is not the actual one, which lies further back and up against the steep SE ridge of Petraficha. The GR11 gains height beforehand to easily reach…

2.50 Collado de Petraficha, 1961m. Go down the obvious valley ahead, E, but look out for the waymarks leading off right from the main track just before the stream takes to a

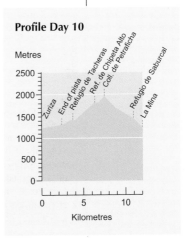

Profile Day 10

Camping: La Mina or a short distance into the next day below the water pipe. The facilities at Selba d'Oza are permanently closed now and the buildings vandalised. There are many places to camp along the Barranco de Petraficha also.

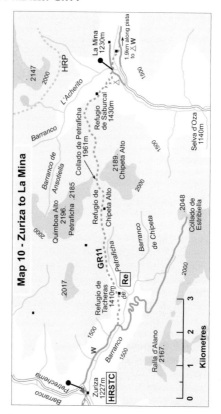

Map 10 - Zuriza to La Mina

narrow ravine. About 1km later, look out for waymarks leading left from the main path. The trail turns SE, passing the old Refugio de Saburcal and snow-depth pole, seen to the left, where the track becomes indistinct on the grass. Continue SE across the grass, soon finding the path again which goes down many zigzags to the open area of…

4.05 La Mina, 1230m. *This is again the staging area for the GR11 as the facilities at Selva d'Oza have closed. New farm buildings have been erected in recent times.*

Buttresses, Alano ridge

La Mina

There are plenty of places to camp. Cross the bridge and take a waymarked path on the right across the pastures to another bridge and access to the pista beyond. Just before the pista, the old refugio still has one usable room up the steps and across planks over a rotten floor. There is a standpipe, on the left of the pista, 1.9km into the Guarrinza valley, with camping possibilities below. It is also possible to reach Aguas Tuertas for an excellent camping situation. However, it appears that cows are now grazed in either the Guarrinza or the Aguas Tuertas valleys.

DAY 11
La Mina – Candanchù

Distance:	22km (13.7 miles)
Height gain:	990m
Height loss:	670m
Time:	6hrs

Maps: Editorial Alpina Candanchù. Prames maps (1:40,000 and 1:50,000) 11.

A long but pleasant day, with an easy walk along the left bank of the Río Aragón Subordan before the route climbs steeply into the long, flat hanging valley of Aguas Tuertas. There is spectacular rough mountain scenery around the Ibón d'Estanés before the route takes a short excursion into France. It then leads back into Spain to the ski complex of Candanchù.

0.00 La Mina, 1130m. Cross the bridge and take the waymarked path on the right across pastures to another bridge and access to the *pista* beyond. Turn

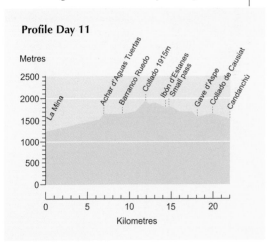

Profile Day 11

Camping: At the Achar and Barranco de la Rueda end of the Aguas Tuertas, just before the pass at 1915m and in the small hanging valley above Ibón Estanés. Also at Camping Canfranc, with restaurant and camping gas supplies, situated 3km beyond Candanchù.

left, E, into the Guarrinza valley, which seems to be filled with all the cows of Spain during the summer and which also contains the Río Aragon Subordan. It turns ESE, easily ascending the left side of the valley. A water point is reached 1.9km along the *pista*, and after 7km the *pista* makes a long loop westwards, while the GR11 climbs steeply

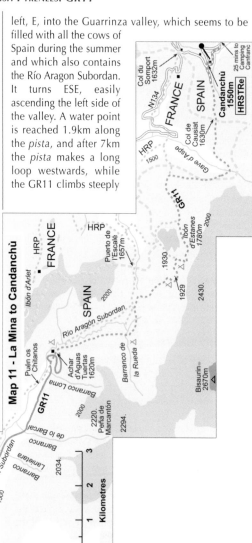

Map 11 - La Mina to Candanchù

ESE to the narrow opening to the hanging valley above called...

Looking back to the Petraficha ridge

1.40 Achar d'Aguas Tuertas, 1620m. *Entrance to the long water meadow of Aguas Tuertas that is very wet at snow melt times. A quite delightful place. The hut here may not be usable any more.* Follow the rocky path S, which leads to the flat valley. Follow a faint trail and waymarks, slightly east of south, always on the true right (west) of the valley, to the crossing of the Barranco de la Rueda and dry ground. *A 'sock' crossing in May!* Here, turn E towards the Puerto de l'Escalé, which lies at the end of the grassy area and some 2km away. After about 10–15mins keep a look out for waymarks leading off right across grass, SE from the main path. Continue SE, climbing up a well-marked trail to a small pass that gains access to the Ibón Estanés valley...

3.25 Collado, 1915m. Go down NE, at first, following the marks towards and well above the western end of the lake, and at about 1800m take the right branch of the path, SSW, across a small hanging valley, turning eastwards to the SE end of the lake called...

4.15 Ibón d'Estanés, 1780m. From the end of the lake, go up E to another small pass, 1810m, going down NE on the other side, on the left side of the valley, to a grassy place at about 1680m, where the HRP leaves to the left. The GR11 turns right, S, over a grassy rise, gently descending into France near to the border marker No.293, some 40m to the left. The route follows the border for a while, then goes into the beech wood and turns SE to go down to cross the Gave d'Aspe at about 1560m. Traverse, with great care, a very steep earth and scree slope, caused by a landslide, and then follow the path NE and E out of the wood to the wide pass of…

5.40 Col de Causiat, 1630m. *Border again, back into Spain with the ski resort below. Signpost to Ibón Estanés.* Continue E passing between two hollows down to the road that brings you past the Alpine Military School to…

6.00 Candanchù, 1550m. *Hotels, restaurants, bars and telephones do not seem to function during the summer. You arrive at a sharp bend in the main road through the resort. Up and left goes to the Collado de Somport and the main road into France. A couple of hundred metres up this road, on the right, is the only shop, with bar, that sells provisions during the spring. Other places may open during the summer or at weekends. By going down right, E, and taking the first turning on the right that bends to the SW, you will reach the Refugio-Albergues Valle de Aragón and El Aguila on the left. El Aguila may open only during the evening during some weeks in June and possibly one week in September, as resident guardians go on holiday.*

DAY 12
Candanchù – Sallent de Gállego

Distance:	22.3km (13.9 miles)
Height gain:	880m
Height loss:	1125m
Time:	6hrs 10mins

Maps: Editorial Alpina Candanchù and Panticosa. Prames maps (1:40,000 and 1:50,000) 14.

From Candanchù there are two GR11 routes to Sallent de Gállego. The recommended one is through the Canal Roya valley and Anayet lakes area, and this is the one described here. It is a superb walk, with plenty of opportunities to camp as required. At the head of the valley the path surprisingly surmounts a ring of steep, broken crags, winding along grassy fault lines to join the Anayet lakes where Pic du Midi d'Ossau towers to the north in France.

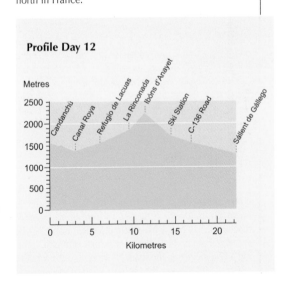

Profile Day 12

Camping: Plenty of places from above the Lacuas hut to the *pista*. There is also a campsite at Sallent de Gállego and another below the entrance to the Canal Roya valley. This can be reached by following the yellow GR65 variant and GR11 Canal Izas marks down to a road. Turn left, cross a bridge, and Camping Canfranc will be found up and on the left.

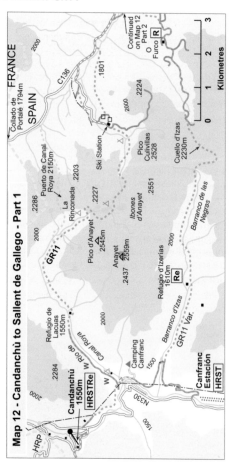

Map 12 - Candanchù to Sallent de Gallego - Part 1

0.00 Candanchù, 1550m. From the *refugio* El Aguila go down the road which turns E to join another before reaching the N-330, where there is a GR11 notice. Cross the main road and take the *pista*, which climbs SE, starting a few metres up the road, N, and passes by a hut to reach a little pass. This is part of the Santiago de

Compostela trail variant, which goes down the left side of the river. The trail climbs over two earthen banks and down some steps before turning E into the Canal Roya. It passes under power lines to join the *pista* that comes up from the road below, and shortly comes to the junction with the other GR11 route to Sallent via Collado de Izas, where the Santiago trail also turns off to the right. *Take this turn for Camping Canfranc.* A few metres on is the spring and picnic area of…

0.35 Merendero de Canal Roya, 1360m. *Wild camping possible below.* Follow the *pista* into the Canal Roya, NE. After about 1km a water point is reached, and 1km later the *pista* becomes a path leading to, at about 1550m, a bridge over the stream just below…

1.20 Refugio de Lacuas, 1550m. *Probably unusable by now.* Continue along the true left side of the stream, crossing one from the Anayet peaks on the right. At 1800m the track is joined from the left by the path from the Coll du Portalet on the frontier via the Puerto de Canal Roya to the north. However, continue along the left side of the main stream, turning SE to enter the area below the crags called…

Pic du Midi d'Ossau, from Ibóns d'Anayet

Map 12 - Candanchù to Sallent de Gállego - Part 2

Kilometres
0 1 2 3

Embalse de la Sarra 1438m

.2295 Peña Foratata

Formigal 1550m
HRSTRe

2000

Barranco de Pondiellos

1500

Sallent de Gállego 1305m
HRSTC

R

Embalse de Gallego 1496m
C-136
1500

Embalse de Lanuza 1238m

Pazino 1965

1442

2.45 La Rinconada, 1870m. Follow the trail to the waymark at the start of the climb, on the left side of the valley. In season, especially at weekends, walkers descending the route will indicate the start. Otherwise it becomes apparent as one approaches the left-hand side of the lowest part of the crags. Once on the crag follow the path as it clings to the steep rocks. Later, as the route becomes less clear, surmount the last hump in a SE direction to reach the…

3.40 Ibóns d'Anayet, 2227m. *An idyllic and popular spot. The mountain to the north is the Pic du Midi d'Ossau.* The way down to the Barranco Culibillas is to the SE, where it soon becomes apparent as the last grassy moraine is topped. *The mountains then seen in the distance framed by the crags of the valley are the Infiernos, whose pass on the left side carries the GR11 towards Panticosa.* However, to matters at hand, go down the Culibillas valley crossing the stream three times, until finally keeping to its right side. The path soon joins the…

4.25 Pista, 1770m. This now goes down to the new Formigal ski station, where a road continues down to the Corral de las Mulas below the C-136 road. The new ski station has obliterated the old route. The GR11 has been routed down the left-hand side of the road. Cross the bridge below both parking areas and follow paint marks on powerline poles. The vague path turns away from the powerlines coming close to the road and then drops down to a *pista*. Turn right and follow to the road, about 120m from the lower bridge. Climb the road to the main C-136 road. *The old GR11 is still waymarked, but little used now. The following instructions are for those who wish to use the old GR11 way, but the boulder fields are* hard work and it is no longer recommended. Go right across the first large car-park area and turn NNW down the pista, behind rock mound, for 45m. A bearing of ENE across the hollow leads to waymarks. Contour the steep hillside ahead, just below the height of the parking area, to locate the first waymarks on one of the tracks that cross the hillside. Follow waymarks across two boulder fields and down steep grass to a bridge over the Gallego river, thus joining the C-136.

5.05 C-136 road, 1550m. From the Corral de las Mulas go down the road for 2.3km, passing the road turning to Formigal and Sallent *(petrol station with restaurant on the right)*, taking a farm track to the left just before another bridge over the river. This goes down to Sallent, with short-cuts crossing the road a few times before arriving at…

6.10 Sallent de Gállego, 1305m. *Hotels, restaurants, bars, shops, bank, telephone. The municipal campsite is still in use. As the town is reached, there is a small* supermercado, *just after the upper bridge, to the left, with the youth hostel Albergue Foratata on the right.*

DAY 13
Sallent de Gállego –
Refugio de Respomuso

Maps: Editorial
Alpina
Panticosa/Formigal.
Prames maps
(1:40,000 and
1:50,000) 15. The
profile and map in
the Spanish guide
are incorrect in
distance and height
and the new *refugio*
is shown at the side
of the wrong stream.

Distance:	11.8km (7.3 miles)
Height gain:	925m
Height loss:	30m
Time:	3hrs 45mins

The climb today emerges into stunning mountain scenery – an absolutely delightful place. Please note that in early June snow may make passing the lake on either side hazardous. If this is so, it may also make the crossing of the Collado de Tebarray difficult or impossible. The new *refugio* can be used if you are without a tent, but those with camping kit will relish the high camps with stunning scenery. Balneario de Panticosa lies just 8.5km away to the east of Sallent, on the other side of a 3000m ridge. The GR11 takes a sweeping curve to the north following the Río Aguas Limpias to cross the ridge coming from the Grande Fache, 3005m, in the NE on the border with France. At Balneario de Panticosa there is nowhere to re-provision, but a picnic lunch can be ordered at the *refugio*.

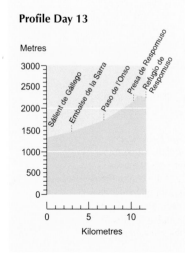

Profile Day 13

Metres

Sallent de Gállego
Embalse de la Sarra
Paso de l'Onso
Presa de Respomuso
Refugio de Respomuso

Kilometres

0.00 Sallent de Gállego, 1305m. *A new route has been opened, using an ancient track that climbs to the road below the Embalse de la Sarra.* Leave by NE of town, keeping to the western side of the river. Continue along the *pista*, ignoring a turn left after about 1km. Then after a minute

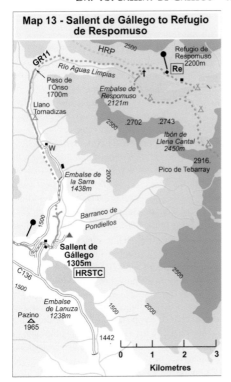

Map 13 - Sallent de Gállego to Refugio de Respomuso

Camping: Llano Tornadizas, around Respomuso (super spot at the head of the lake), and below or beside Ibón de Llena Cantal, about 1hr 15mins into the next day.

or so turn left up the ancient track and follow to the road. Turn right, and just before the dam take the track to the left of the Sarra lake…

0.35 Embalse de La Sarra, 1438m. *Bar/restaurant reported at northern end of reservoir, but not seen by author.* Follow the track on the western side of the lake, passing picnic site with water supply at the end of the lake. Continue, NNW, to follow the *pista* upwards. In about 1km, a grassy area beside the stream is passed, on the right. *This is Llano Tornadizas, suitable for a wild camp.* The trail continues north with the stream down to the right. The valley narrows at…

1.55 Paso de l'Onso, 1700m. The trail gradually turns towards the east, with Llano Cheto, a grassy area, down below to the right through the trees. Continue climbing E, a seemingly never-ending trail, until quite suddenly the enormous dam of Respomuso looms high overhead. *It is possible to find a path climbing to the southern end of the dam. At the base of the steps, turn right through the concrete structures until the path can be seen. The final climb takes to the steps up to the...*

3.25 Presa de Respomuso, 2121m. *The chapel is called Capella de la Virgin de las Nieves. To avoid the refugio, cross the dam (the No Access sign refers to when works were being carried out). Take good care in high winds, as the wind velocity increases dramatically as it is funnelled through the gap in the centre, over which an iron walkway takes pedestrians to the other side. Follow the track around the south of the lake until it is possible to turn right, SSE, into the Llena Cantal valley that is beyond the eastern end of the lake. It is possible to camp in this valley or climb up the next steep section to Ibón de Llena Cantal.*

To visit or stay at the new *refugio*, climb the zigzags above the chapel. The path goes ENE after the buildings and climbs back W for a while, avoiding the path going straight on, before turning E, well above the lake, which goes all the way to...

3.45 Refugio de Respomuso, 2200m. *Open all year, some supplies are available.*

DAY 14
Refugio de Respomuso –
Balneario de Panticosa

Distance:	13.3km (8.3 miles)
Height gain:	690m
Height loss:	1250m
Time:	5hrs 25mins

Maps: Editorial Alpina Panticosa/ Formigal. Prames maps (1:40,000 and 1:50,000) 15.

A truly alpine stage today. The huge complex bulk of Balaitús is revealed to the north as height is gained. A snow tongue usually eases the climb to the short, broken gully leading to the knife-edge Collado de Tebarray. The trail brushes past the Infiernos peaks before the easy but long descent to the valley destination. An outstanding experience!

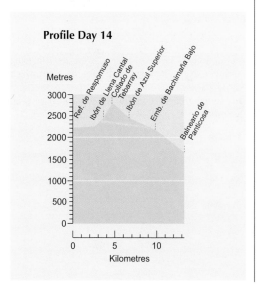

Profile Day 14

Camping: Beside Ibón de Llena Cantal, around the Azul lakes and at the camping area well above Balneario de Panticosa (too far away from the town to use it for meals).

Map 14 - Respomuso to Balneario de Panticosa

Cuello de Infierno and Ibón Azul Superior

0.00 Refugio de Respomuso, 2200m. Take the path going SE from the *refugio*. Follow this past a locked cabin and around the head of the lake. *Excellent camping spot here!* The path turns to the SW to join the GR trail coming around the south side of the lake. Turn SSE into the Llena Cantal valley. Climb the steep section to…

1.25 Ibón de Llena Cantal, 2450m. *The massif to the NNE is that of Balaitús, the summit being 3151m.* The Collado de Tebarray lies to the SE, to the left of the conical peak of Tebarray above to the south. There is usually a snow slope leading to the pass that

Snow slope to Collado de Tebarray

facilitates the first part of the ascent. However, at the end of the summer it will be missing and the climb is arduous over loose moraine debris. A short, steep, broken gully is climbed (be aware that stones may be dislodged by anyone above) to gain the narrow…

2.30 Collado de Tebarray (or Piedrafita), 2782m. *This is about as high as the GR11 gets, only surpassed during day 38.* Go down the very steep slope towards the lake to reach the track contouring SE, well above the lake, to the next pass…

2.45 Cuello d'o Infierno, 2721m. *From here a popular ascent of the Infiernos can be made. The first difficulty*

Bramatuero lakes with Vignemale in the background

can be turned on the right by gaining another ridge further on. Go down the valley to the east, often over snow, passing to the north of the Ibóns Azules, a popular place for a tent. Continue E to reach the large lake of...

3.55 Embalse Bachimaña Alto, 2207m. Cross the stream coming from the Azul lakes and continue SE, with the Bachimana lake on the left. It is important not to go down the left side of this lake. The track turns SW around the north of the lower lake before going steeply down the Caldarés valley, S, passing a small camping area before arriving at...

5.25 Balneario de Panticosa, 1640m. *Guarded hut to the right, Casa de Piedra, open all year, 120 places, bar and meals. Hotels, restaurants, bars and telephone.*

DAY 15
Balneario de Panticosa – San Nicolás de Bujaruelo

Distance:	20.5km (12.7 miles)
Height gain:	940m
Height loss:	1240m
Time:	6hrs 50mins

Maps: Editorial Alpina Panticosa/Formigal, and Valle de Ordesa. Prames maps (1:40,000 and 1:50,000) 16.

Another day to be savoured, passing through the granite wilderness on either side of the Brazato pass. Then, there is the long but easy walk down the Ara valley to Bujaruelo, justifiably popular during the summer for camping and picnicking. One can go further, if desired, to another campsite some 2km down the *pista* or even all the way down to the road at Puente de los Navarros, where there is yet another campsite and another beside

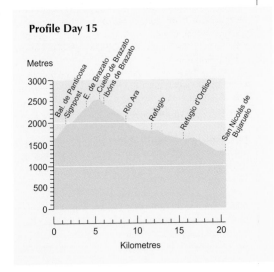

Profile Day 15

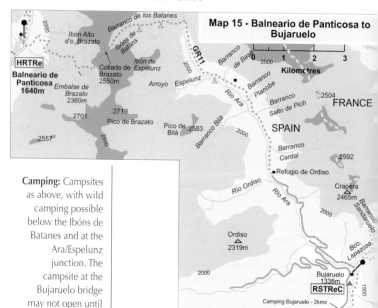

Map 15 - Balneario de Panticosa to Bujaruelo

Camping: Campsites as above, with wild camping possible below the Ibóns de Batanes and at the Ara/Espelunz junction. The campsite at the Bujaruelo bridge may not open until late June.

the hotel, 1km south along the road to Torla. There is a small but comprehensive supermarket at this last site that may still sell basic mountaineering equipment. Careful planning of victualling will be needed at Bujaruelo. In season, during the next four stages, meals can be obtained at Bujaruelo, the campsites below, at the Refugio de Góriz only if in residence, Pineta *refugio*, Parzán and at Góriz. However, supplies can only be obtained with certainty at the campsite below Bujaruelo, the supermarket at the campsite below the Puente de Navarros and at Parzán.

0.00 Balneario de Panticosa, 1640m. From the SE of the town, take the steps that go up SE beside the Casa Belio, which continue to the Fuente de la Saluz, where an old path is followed shortly to take another to the NE. Then, near to an avalanche-retaining wall, take a path on the right, SE, that climbs steeply, zigzagging through the pines to the signpost to Ibones de Labaza and Diens d'os Batans, about 1hr from the town. Do not take this path, but go S to climb a grassy rise to the boulder wilderness. Follow the trail round to the left to climb NE then again SE, crossing the stream coming down from the left from Ibón Alto d'o Brazato. Continue, generally SE to reach the large dammed lake...

2.20 Embalse de Brazato, 2360m. Go round the north end of the lake, then turn N to reach the west shoulder of Pico de Racias above the upper lakes. The pass lies a few hundred metres away to the NE...

3.00 Collado de Brazato, 2550m. *The huge massif ahead is Vignemale, containing in its 3000m horseshoe crest the large and steep Glacier d'Ossoue.* Continue NE down the valley ahead, passing a large grassy area on the right, keeping to the left of the Ibóns de Batanes. Then cross the outlet stream of the last lake to the right side, E, past more granite blocks to easier terrain, eventually to reach the...

4.10 Ara River, 2000m. Cross the river. This can be tricky when it is filled with melt-water or after heavy rain. Above there is a clear path. Turn right and follow past a...

Vignemale from the upper Ara

Head of the Ara

The ancient bridge at Bujaruelo

5.00 Hut, 1800m. *Bad condition in 2003,* but *with water nearby.* Carry on down the track to...

5.50 Refugio d'Ordiso, 1580m. *Dirty and not inviting.* From here a *pista* continues down the left of the valley and is followed, always on the left of the river, all the way to...

6.50 San Nicolás de Bujaruelo, 1338m. *The refugio attached to the bar at Bujaruelo, with full services, has been closed, but may now be open again. The campsite has a new site block with shop and excellent toilets. The path continues on the left, N, of the river, but the refugio/bar/restaurant and campsite are across the medieval bridge. The refugio/bar is open from Easter to the end of October but is expensive. From here a pista goes down the right side of the river to join the path at the Santa Elena bridge. A footbridge has been built across the River Ara, from the GR11 path, to provide access to the campsite/bar restaurant situated 30mins downstream from Bujaruelo. Facilities are good here, including some cheap accommodation at Camping Valle de Bujaruelo, just 30mins from Bujaruelo bridge. There is also a path ENE to the road, in France, at the Port de Gavarnie.*

DAY 16
Bujaruelo – Refugio de Góriz

Distance:	22.5km (14.0 miles)
Height gain:	1180m
Height loss:	360m
Time:	6hrs

This stage leads through canyon country. First the Garganta de Bujaruelo, then the larger Ordesa canyon within the boundary of the Parque National de Ordesa y Monte Perdido. Created in 1918 and extended in 1982 this national park was the vision of one Lucien Briet, captivated by the outstanding beauty of the area, who first visited Ordesa in 1891. Waymarking ceases at the car park and starts again at the little bridge in the Circo de Soasa. Beware, though – GR11-type waymarks appear all around the canyon as marked approach routes. Drink only from the side streams, as the main

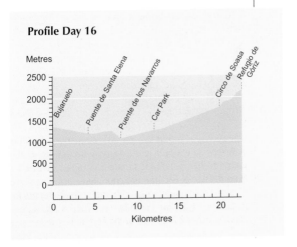

Profile Day 16

Maps: Editorial Alpina Valle de Ordesa. This 1:40,000 map is recommended especially if further walks in the area are anticipated, and it is preferable to the SGE ones or the Editorial Alpina Bigorre. Prames maps (1:40,000 and 1:50,000) 17. New route below Santa Elena bridge not correctly shown on Prames 1:40,000 map. There is no need to climb the 200m, which is really a local scenic route! Neither does it climb the *clavijas* at Soasa.

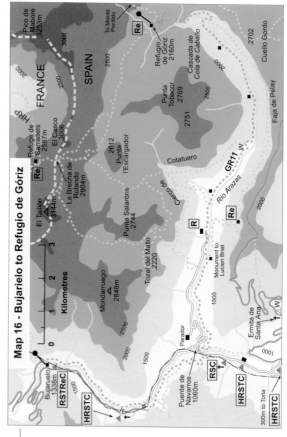

Map 16 - Bujarielo to Refugio de Góriz

Arazas river comes down from the Góriz hut, where the Barranco de Góriz may still be used as a loo by some!

0.00 Bujaruelo, 1338m. *One can follow the pista down to the Santa Elena bridge, passing Camping Valle de Bujaruelo. However, the GR11 follows the left bank of the Ara. From the bar, go back over the bridge, turning right to follow the path S along the left side of the River*

Ara. This wanders through woods past a path on the right, which goes to Camping Valle de Bujaruelo via a small footbridge, to reach the bridge, Puente de Santa Elena, where the *pista* crosses to the path side. *The pista can be followed all the way down to the road. However, the GR11 has now been routed along the western side of the canyon.* From the western side of Puente de Santa Elena take the path ESE that follows the right-hand bank of the Ara. The GR11 does not follow that marked on the map, which is another trail. The trail starts by going downhill and passes a waterfall, seen to the right. About 15mins later it climbs easily about 40m, and climbs a further 10m a little later. About 10–15mins further on a turn left is ignored, and at a grassy patch take the left fork that leads over rocks to a clear trail. *The path going straight on also joins with the clear trail below.* Turn right, WSW, and follow through turns to the road below. Turn left, and after about 200m take the signposted path on the left to the end of the bridge beside…

1.25 Puente de los Navarros, 1060m. *The national park starts here. A new campsite lies 10mins down the road,*

Camping: No camping allowed in the national park, with the exception of the area SE from the Góriz hut, where tents can be erected early evening but must be lowered and held down with rocks during the day. If you don't do it, the guardians will! I have come across a regulation that states that one can bivouac, with or without a tent, above 2100m at Soasa and above 1800m in the Añisclo canyon.

Overlooking the Ordesa canyon to the Circo de Cotatuero

Circo de Soasa

S, with supermarket and bar/restaurant. A further 10mins S is the Hotel and Camping Ordesa, with bar/restaurant and supermarket. In another 2km is the small town of Torla, with all facilities. The national park is closed to private traffic during the summer season. Buses are used from Torla, but they do not pick up walkers en route. A new track, on the right, passes beneath the road to cross the River Arazas by a concrete bridge. Climb up the other side to reach a *pista*, which was the old way to Ordesa before the road was built. Turn left, NE, to follow this track, called the Camino de Turieta Bajo. Although most of the track into and along the canyon is very wide it is marked on the sketch map as a path rather than a *pista* as it only takes foot traffic (apart from any official park vehicles). Continue along this track above the river on the true left of the valley, passing the monument to Lucien Briet opposite the Puente de Ordesa, to another bridge, Puente de las Fuentes. *It is possible to miss this, as tree growth has obscured the road and waymarks lead towards the Senda de Cazadores that climbs the south wall of the canyon.* Cross over the Arazas here to the road just before the...

El Cilindro (on the way to Monte Perdido from the Góriz hut)

*Brêche de Roland
(Excursion from
Góriz)*

2.25 Ordesa car park, 1300m. *Large bar/restaurant on
the left.* Go along the wide and popular path E on the
right side of the river, climbing easy slopes that steepen
somewhat past the cascades to the open space of the
Circo de Soasa. *The large waterfall at the head of the
valley is called Cascada de Cola de Caballo, the 'horse
tail falls'.* Continue NE towards the falls until a small
footbridge allows the crossing of the river at...

4.35 Circo de Soasa, 1760m. On the right, E, will be
seen a large scree slope with a path winding up it. This is
the way to easily gain the first shelf above the canyon
and the way of the GR11. The adventurous, if they wish,
can climb out by the iron rods (*las clavijas*) found in the
obvious cave to the right of the falls. Once above the
canyon wall follow the trail upward, NW and then
NNW, through slopes of English irises, in season, over
easy rock steps and grassy terraces to...

6.00 Refugio de Góriz, 2160m. *Open all year, 96 places,
meals service, water point and camping area. The climb
NE from here to Monte Perdido, third highest in the
Pyrenees, is spectacular but easy. A late start is required
to allow the snow to soften. It is a long but rewarding trip
through snow-filled hanging valleys with seemingly no*

easy exit, but one is always found. One has nothing but admiration for those who first worked out this way to the top. The famous Brêche de Roland (Breca Rolán) is another popular excursion from here. Please note that there is good grass and water just below the Collado d'Arrablo, but this is still within the boundary of the national park. I am informed that the watercourse here is very sparse in high summer.

DAY 17
Refugio de Góriz – Circo de Pineta

Maps: Editorial Alpina Valle de Ordesa. Prames maps (1:40,000 and 1:50,000) 18. There is not a GR waymarked route either to or from the Pineta Refugio to the Circo, as shown on the Prames 1:40,000 map.

Camping: Circo de Pineta

Distance:	13.5km (8.4 miles)	Variant:
		11.5km (7.1 miles)
Height gain:	880m	590m
Height loss:	1750m	1460m
Time:	7hrs 10mins	6hrs 40mins

The GR11 used to make its way around the south side of Sum de Ramond (la Punta d'as Olas) via ledges and gullies – some very narrow and dangerous in snow. It is essential to enquire at the Góriz hut or at the Parador Hotel in the Pineta valley, if coming from that direction, to ascertain the condition of the route, if you wish to use it. It is also important to assess whether you or your party are comfortable scrambling with such exposure across the upper wall of the Añisclo canyon. There is a stainless steel chain to assist in the awkward exit from the gully. Nevertheless, this is a superb route if the above conditions are met.

As more and more walkers are taking to this mountain area, in 1989 a second, easier, route was waymarked into the Añisclo canyon below a water spout called the Fuén Blanca, from where the route climbs out to join the first route at the Añisclo pass. The original route via the high ledges is now the variant. Both routes are described here, as the Añisclo canyon route has

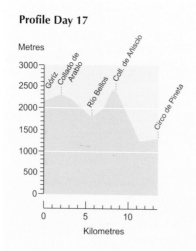

Profile Day 17

Metres

3000 — Góriz, Collado de Arablo, Coll. de Añisclo
2500 — Río Bellos
2000 —
1500 — Circo de Pineta
1000 —
500 —
0 —

0   5   10
Kilometres

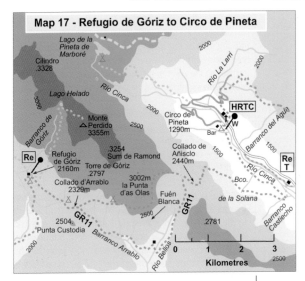

Map 17 - Refugio de Góriz to Circo de Pineta

changed from being an optional extra to an essential alternative stage, and now has become the safest and officially recognised route. Officially, the stage now ends at the Refugio de Pineta, situated on the other side of the road, opposite Barranco Castiecho.

0.00 Refugio de Góriz, 2160m. Take the path SE from the hut, which ascends gradually to reach…
0.30 Collado de Arrablo, 2329m. For the Añisclo canyon route, take the path SE going down, with the Barranco Arrablo to the left. Continue along the SW edge of the gorge for about 400m until cairns and waymarks lead the way over the edge and down the first crag. **Note:** *Care is needed in descending the rock steps, though these are not difficult.* Go right on the wide grassy shelf and follow the way down. Later, after another rock band, the trail crosses the stream to the left side. This can be difficult during snowmelt conditions or after heavy rain. Steep zigzags lead down, past the Fuén Blanca seen to the left, through lush undergrowth past a cabin to…

1.45 the valley floor, 1800m. Cross the Río Vellos by a small bridge, turn left, NE, and commence the climb, on the left side of the valley. This is not difficult, but seems very tiring on the steeper parts. Much higher the track crosses to the right of the stream and with many zigzags surmounts the final steep section, turning E, crossing the slope, to reach…

4.00 Collado de Añisclo, 2440m. *The first view of the descent can be quite intimidating. However the way down uses a shallow depression which removes much of the sense of exposure. Great care must be taken not to get lost on the descent. In particular, do not try to reach the Parador below on a direct line by continuing the early direction of the descent.* Go steeply down NE by zigzags over rocky ground to about 1900m where a path goes off to the left, NW, along the Faja Tormosa, signposted. Do not take this path. Go down E over more bands (some scrambling required) into the wood, now travelling SE. Take care to maintain the correct route, as avalanche debris often crosses the trail. The Barranco Castiecho is crossed before turning NW again. *If the* refugio *is the planned destination, continue down the path, NE, to join a* pista, *NNW. Cairns and yellow paint marks lead across a meadow and river debris, N, to cross two streams of the River Zinca by stepping stones and then tree bridge. There is a bar and telephone at the* refugio. Otherwise, go NW, passing beneath a rocky outcrop, to go along the right side of the valley to the camping area at…

7.10 Circo de Pineta, 1290m. *Hotel, telephone, camping area with small bar, GR11 notice-board with map and water points near to bar and behind the chapel. This is the Capella de Nuestra Senora de Pineta, originally Romanesque and restored during the 17th century. The road goes down 13km to Bielsa to meet the road to Parzán, the Bielsa tunnel and France. If the bar is closed, drinks and meals can be obtained at the Parador.*

Variant – the higher route
0.30 Collado de Arrablo, 2329m. Turn NE along an easily ascending, well-waymarked, wide and stony

Circo de Pineta

sloping ledge. Climbing from this the route passes two waterfalls and most suitable camping spots. It climbs again, passing a narrow ledge turning N around the buttress at the end of the SE ridge of Sum de Ramond, which is called Punta d'as Olas. *A path goes off left here, presumably to the top of the Punta d'as Olas.* A little later the trail enters a rocky gully with stainless steel chain high up for snow conditions. Go up this for 40m distance. On the right the chain assists in climbing from the gully to the steep descent. Go down this until a boulder-filled gully to the left allows access to yet another ledge going downhill. Care must be taken again as this narrows. Another cable assists with safety. Continue down SE towards the Collado de Añisclo, passing to the south of a little hill that divides the pass in two, to reach…

3.30 Collado de Añisclo, 2440m. Continue as described in the main route, above.

The narrow ridge at la Brêche (Excursion from Góriz) (Day 16)

DAY 18
Circo de Pineta – Parzán

Distance:	18km (11.2 miles)
Height gain:	880m
Height loss:	1025m
Time:	5hrs 25mins

Maps: Editorial Alpina Valle de Ordesa. Prames maps (1:40,000 and 1:50,000) 19.

The highlight of this day is the view of the Perdido massif from the NE rim of the Pineta valley and the descent route of yesterday. Then the way is down the Río Real valley over rough *pista* then road to Parzán.

Camping: Apart from any camping opportunities higher up, there is no campsite at Parzán.

0.00 Circo de Pineta, 1290m. Take the path going up N through the wood, which starts behind the chapel beside the water point. Be careful to find the diagonally ascending path – do not follow the one that goes straight up.

Profile Day 18

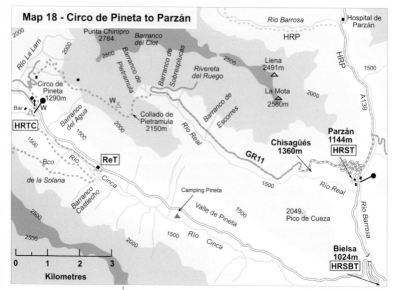

Map 18 - Circo de Pineta to Parzán

Cross loops of the *pista*, coming from La Larri and curving around the head of the Pineta valley, to reach the flat area of...

0.45 La Larri, 1560m. Just after the farm hut, take the track going NE. Do not follow a waymark into the streambed but cross a little higher to almost reach the Barranco Opacas. Here the trail turns SE to climb through a few zigzags to reach easier ground. Stunning views! Continue SE, with scant marking, below a hut seen high to the left, to reach a distinct flat grassy area bordered by small crags. *Camping possible here.* Cross this depression SE and in about 12–15mins climb E to the...

3.10 Collado de Pietramula, 2150m. Go down, N then NE, then down zigzags, through large boulders and ENE to cross the Río Real. Go up the left bank to gain the *pista* and follow it down the left of the valley, SE then NE, to the road past the village of...

4.55 Chisagües, 1360m. Continue along the road, then down many zigzags, turning right, then right again into...

5.25 Parzán, 1144m. *This is just off the main road from Bielsa, some 3km to the south, which continues north to go through the Bielsa tunnel to France. Bar/restaurant and small supermarket beside service station on the main road. Hostal La Fuén, with restaurant, is also on the main road, south of the filling station, on the opposite side of the road, tel: 974.50.10.47. Casa Marión, in the village has rooms, tel: 974.50.11.90. A footpath connects the village with the* hostal.

DAY 19
Parzán – Viadós

Maps: Editorial
Alpina Bachimala.
Prames maps
(1:40,000 and
1:50,000) 20.

Distance:	19.5km (12.1 miles)
Height gain:	1445m
Height loss:	850m
Time:	6hrs

This pleasant day, mostly *pista* at first, passes through a
gorge along the Barranco de Urdiceto. Then the route
traverses the wide grassy pass of Los Caballos below the
large dammed lake of Urdiceto. The trail goes down to
farmland, dominated on the right by Punta Suelza. It
rises three times before picking up a *pista* again down to
the large open area of Es Plans beside the Cinqueta river.
Supplies will be needed until the campsite shop in the
Esera valley is reached.

Profile Day 19

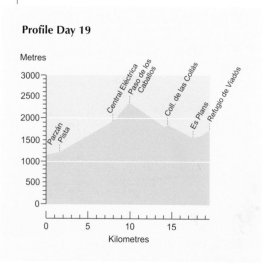

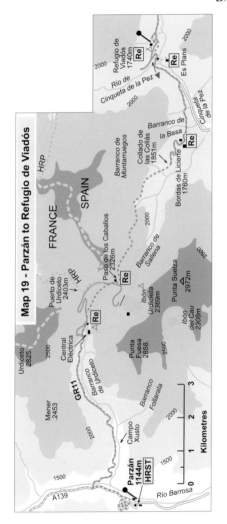

Map 19 - Parzán to Refugio de Viadós

Camping: Near to cabin above Central Eléctrica de Ordiceto. Beside the two smaller lakes above the Caballos pass to the south or at the far end of Es Plans and above the unmanned *refugio*. This campsite is open only from 1st July to 21st August. It has a bar/restaurant and cheap rooms.

0.00 Parzán, 1144m. Leave the village by the main road going north passing by the GR11 notice-board at the

Punta Suelza, seen to the south of the route

turning to Chisagüés, and in about 1.5km turn right at the sign to Ordiceto. *Here a variant of the High Level Route joins from the north.* Follow the *pista* upwards along the right side of the Ordiceto or Pardina stream, first SE, then E, then NE and E again. A short-cut across one of the bends in the *pista* can be taken just before…

2.15 Central Eléctrica de Urdiceto, 1940m. *Small cabin above the small lake suitable for overnight stop with camping spot nearby.* Continue along the *pista* for about 1.2km, until it starts to zigzag steeply, where a track is taken to the right, SE, which climbs nearer to the valley floor to…

3.20 Paso de los Caballos, 2326m. *New small stone hut on left of track. The trail can be seen ahead, SE, crossing a ridge coming down from the north. The* pista *continues SW to the lake.* Follow the track E, at first, then SE to cross the ridge. Go down E to a grassy level where the track turns left, N then NE, to pass a small cabin. Go down the right side of the Barranco de Montarruegos (or Mantarruegas), then cross to the left bank. Continue SE through a small wood to the meadows of Sallena and a rough hut. Go SE through pines to a wide path, crossing the Barranco de la Basa. Climb SSE then ESE to the…

4.45 Collado de las Collás, 1851m. Go down the zigzags of the new *pista*, passing a hut on the right, now open and suitable for an overnight stop. Continue down the *pista* to the area of farm buildings around the *pista* known as Bordas de Licierte. Turn left, E, along the *pista* that goes down to join another larger one coming from the right, up the Cinqueta valley. Follow this NNE to the large flat grassy area of…

5.20 Es Plans, 1550m. *No longer a camping area. There is a hut with 20 places, further up, sometimes with group camping. Just beyond the hut and over the bridge is the new campsite, only open for two months in the summer.* Continue to Viadós by crossing the Rio Cinqueta de la Pez, E, just after the junction with the Añes Cruces branch. Follow the *pista* until a path on the left, near a building, allows access to a short-cut climbing E and crossing the *pista* twice before reaching…

6.00 Refugio de Viadós, 1740m. *The owners, Señor Cazarra and his wife, are very helpful. Meals, drinks and a capacity of about 40 places. Open weekends after Easter and 15th June to 25th of September.*

DAY 20
Viadós – Refugio d'Estós

Maps: Editorial Alpina Posets. Prames maps (1:40,000 and 1:50,000) 21.

Distance:	11.5km (7.1 miles)
Height gain:	860m
Height loss:	710m
Time:	4hrs 15mins

Camping: Plan d'Añes Cruces. No camping below Estós hut nowadays.

This is a short day in order to savour the lovely valleys of Añes Cruces and Estós. It can easily be extended to reach the campsites at Puente de Sant Jaime or Benasque, if desired. Once the Puerto de Gistaín is reached, the massif of the Maladeta can be seen to the east. This contains the highest summit in the Pyrenees, Pico de Aneto, at 3404m. The Pico de Posets lies south from the pass but is not attainable from here – the Barranco d'Estós would have to be followed upwards to the Collado de La Paúl. The position of the Estós hut cannot be seen from the pass, as it is around the right bend in the valley and over the wooded ridge seen just before the two white buildings low in the valley. It can, however, be identified from the far right-hand side of the pass.

Profile Day 20

0.00 Viadós, 1740m. From the hut, take the wide track E through the farm buildings. *The official path, above and to the left, becomes overgrown and ends at a small landslide.* The *pista* becomes a path easily ascending NE along the west (right) side of the valley of the Cinqueta d'Añes Cruces. A short steep ascent to the left avoids a difficult section by a stream before reaching a junction of streams...

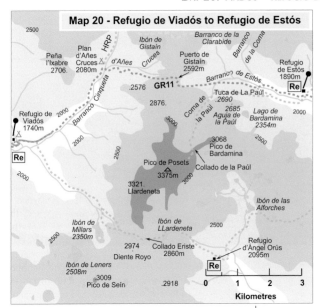

Map 20 - Refugio de Viadós to Refugio de Estós

1.10 Plan d'Añes Cruces, 2080m. Go up the obvious path climbing steeply E on the true left of the stream. This eases, eventually, to climb more gently to…

2.35 Puerto de Gistaín, 2592m. *The French border lies a short distance away to the north along the ridge to Pico de la Madera. Beside the trail to the south lies a curiosity, a stone tube filled with quartz.* Go across the pass, S, past the curiosity, following traces of a path. Go down over scree in a wide channel on the right of the valley. Usually this means making a descending traverse of the steep snow slope to reach easier ground and the Barranco d'Estós, which is crossed for a while before gaining the left bank at the Barranco de Clarabide junction. Keep to the higher trail if the Refugio d'Estós is the target.

4.15 Refugio d'Estós, 1890m. *Open all year. Excellent bar and meals service. About 200 places in two-tier dormitories. Self-catering kitchen. Very popular as it can*

The Maladeta Range beyond the Estós valley

be reached from a car park just above the *Puente de Sant Jaime*. It is mainly supplied by packhorse from the end of the pista at *Cabana del Turmo*.

DAY 21
Estós – Refugio del Puente de Coronas

Distance:	18.5km (11.5 miles)
Height gain:	740m
Height loss:	650m
Time:	5hrs 10mins

Maps: Editorial Alpina Posets and Maladeta. Prames maps (1:40,000 and 1:50,000) 21and 22.

A delightful stroll down the Estós valley and then into the narrow entrance to the Vallibierna, which climbs to the south of the Maladeta massif, with the highest mountain of the Pyrenees, Pico de Aneto, at 3404m, above the head of the valley. Most of the traffic to the summit is from the north, so any ascent from the south would be especially rewarding. **Note:** There is no certainty of provisions after Camping Aneto and Benasque, below Puente de Sant Jaime, until reaching Espot. Meals may

Camping: It is possible to camp, overnight only, below the Batisielles stream. Camping Aneto, Ixeia at Puente de Jaime, and Plan de Senarta.

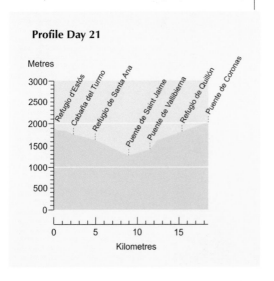

Profile Day 21

127

be had at the Hospital de Viella, which has been refurbished and is now known as Refugi de Sant Nicalau, or at the Restanca, Colomers and Amitges huts, but there is no guarantee of bread or other essentials being available. This means that sufficient food for four and a half days will need to be acquired and carried. It is possible to return to France from Puente de Sant Jaime via the Puerto de Benasque to Luchon by continuing along the *pista*, from the Vallibierna turnoff. Then go up the road to the

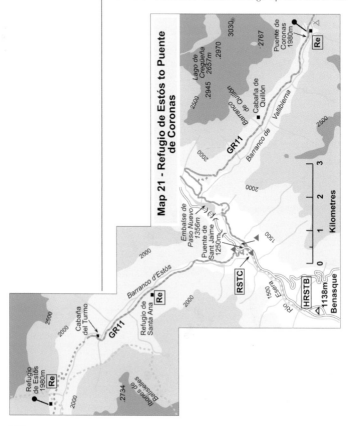

Map 21 - Refugio de Estós to Puente de Coronas

Baños de Benasque and then take a path from the car park to Hospital de Benasque, thus avoiding a long road walk. I understand that there is an infrequent bus service from Camping Aneto to the valley head, which would save about 3–4hrs of walking. Walking the whole distance would take about 9–10hrs without stops. There is a hut on the French side of the pass, which has meals service in season, but camping is no longer allowed by the lakes.

Puerto de Oô, approach to Estós

Benasque

0.00 Refugio d'Estós, 1890m. Go down eastwards along the left of the valley by an obvious path, avoiding a track to the left as the main route zigzags down. The route crosses the river by a bridge just before the start of the *pista* at the Cabaña del Turmo, where the Estós guides pick up supplies. Continue down the *pista* on the right of the valley past the new Santa Ana cabin (10–15 places). Later, the *pista* crosses to the right again and goes down more steeply to the steps above the car park. The steps and then the *pista* lead to the road below. However, the GR11 goes down the path ahead. This is now overgrown, so continue down the *pista* zigzags and take a *pista* on the right, just before the road, which leads into the Camping Aneto grounds at…

1.50 Puente de Sant Jaime, 1250m. *There are two campsites here – Ixeia, north of the bridge, and Aneto, south of the bridge. There are a small supermarket and bar/restaurant at Camping Aneto (opens 15th June each year). Benasque, with all services and mountain equipment shop, is some 3km to the south via an old waymarked trail, on the west of the road, from Camping Aneto. There is a bus service in the summer. A pista leaves Camping Aneto to the north, going under the*

Refugio de Santa Anna

Leaving the Estós hut

bridge. This joins with the *pista* starting on the eastern side of the bridge. Follow the *pista* up the left of the Río Esera, NNE, and when this starts to zigzag, beside the dam of Paso Nuevo, take the path, E, that climbs through the wood and a field to reach the *pista* again. Continue N along the *pista*, crossing the…

2.50 Puente de Vallibierna, 1369m. Continue along the *pista* to where the GR11 turns right, SE, at a signpost. *A short distance ahead, N, is the camping area, with bar, of Plan de Senarta. It is very busy in the holiday season.* Turn SE and climb the *pista* into the Vallibierna valley. The *pista* bears round to the left, and after about 300m keep a look out on the right for a clear, waymarked, steep track that will short-cut a long loop of the *pista*. Go up this, SE, and join the *pista* again in about 15–20mins. Turn right, SSE, along the *pista*, passing the…

4.10 Refugio de Quillón, 1790m. Small hut of six places. Continue SE along the *pista* to the…

5.10 Puente de Coronas, 1980m. *Just after the bridge is a hut with about 14 places. No camping allowed here any more. It is very busy over weekends, when a stay should be avoided. NE from here an ascent to the Collado de Coronas and Aneto can be made.*

DAY 22
*Puente de Coronas –
Hospital de Viella*

Distance:	19.5km (12.1 miles)
Height gain:	1070m
Height loss:	1420m
Time:	7hrs 45mins

Maps: Editorial
Alpina Maladeta and
La Ribagorça.
Prames maps
(1:40,000 and
1:50,000) 22and 23.

Wild and rough country lies ahead, bejewelled with glistening glacial lakes and pools. Once over the Collado (Colladeto) de Riu Bueno the trail wanders down past lakes, passing the Refugio d'Anglós and then continues steeply down through a beech wood into the remote Salenques valley, where a way has been cut through debris from a huge avalanche. Low cloud could make route finding difficult. The Hospital de Viella has

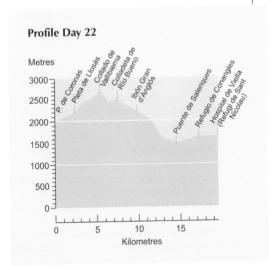

Profile Day 22

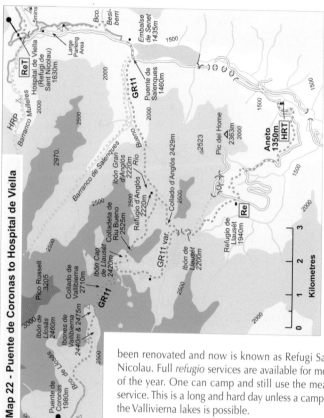

Map 22 - Puente de Coronas to Hospital de Viella

been renovated and now is known as Refugi Sant Nicolau. Full *refugio* services are available for most of the year. One can camp and still use the meals service. This is a long and hard day unless a camp at the Vallivierna lakes is possible.

0.00 Puente de Coronas, 1980m. Go ESE along the *pista* to the junction with the Barranco de Llosas where it turns NE along the right-hand bank and becomes rough and stony. Cross the stream at the grassy area of Pleta de Llosás to climb the right of stream, with waymarked track to...

1.30 Ibón Inferior de Vallibierna, 2440m. *Camping spot above western end of lake, beside small stream.* Go E round the north of the lake turning S to cross the entry stream (dry). Go up the rocky ledges ahead, ESE, passing to the S of the high spot. Continue E climbing down a steep section (not difficult) to a rocky depression and the SE end of the Ibón Superior. Care is needed here to select the correct line. Slightly north of east goes to the Collado dels Bocados, which is to the north of Cap de Llausét and into the head of the Salenques valley. The GR11 climbs E then ESE to the south of Cap de Llausét, which lies ESE from the upper lake. Go up by large boulders and snow to…

2.50 Collado de Vallibierna, 2710m. Go down E at first to a rocky combe, probably snow filled, then SE through

Camping: Beside the two Vallibierna lakes. Beside Ibón Cap de Llauset or above Refugio d'Anglós. Camping zone near to the Conangles hut and in the Conangles valley.

Pleta de Llosas camp

Ibones d'Anglós

rocky terraces and finally grass ledges to a stream at the…

3.25 GR11 Junction, 2410m. *Contouring an obvious line to the left from just above the stream can save a little effort. The right branch goes S to Ibón de Llausét and then NE to Refugio d'Anglós, or continues from the Llausét lake SE to the Refugio de Llausét and on to the small village of Aneto, where there is a bar/restaurant and hotel.* Turn left, NE, up the right of the stream, crossing it near the top, to reach the NW end of the Ibón de Cap de Llausét. Go S along the west of the lake turning E past its southern end. Then, climb SE to the…

3.55 Colladeta de Riu Bueno, 2525m. Go down, SE, passing the first two small lakes, the Ibonets de la Cap d'Anglós, on their right side. The third lake is passed on its left side and then a fourth on the right side. Then continue down through grass to the Ibones d'Anglós, passing between lake Obago to the SW and lake del Mig to the NE. Cross the connecting stream to join the path coming from the Collado d'Anglós. Follow the waymarks that lead towards the NE, with the hut seen a short distance to the left at the WSW end of the Ibón Gran d'Anglós…

4.45 Refugio d'Anglós, 2220m. *A shepherds' hut, often locked.* Go round the right side of the lake and descend on the right of the stream, E, going through a small section of pine trees before turning NE to drop steeply down and through a beech wood to the Barranc de les Salenques. Pass through the avalanche debris and continue along the right of the Salenques stream. The last part can be overgrown with vegetation. The metal bridge below the main road, the N-230, has been washed away, so a crossing of the river cannot be made. Climb to the right of the road-bridge in the Noguera Ribagorzana valley called…

6.25 Puente de Salenques, 1460m. *Border between Aragon and Cataluña. In order to keep off the main road as much as possible, the old route used to cross the road, E, and in about 70m to go down right to pick up the remains of the old road coming from the Embalse de Senet. However, it is preferable to cross the crash barrier and walk along beside it for most of the way to the hut some 200m ahead (GR11 notice-board).* Go past the hut in order to cross the Ribagorzana river by a concrete bridge, on the right. On the other side go left up the *pista*, N, now waymarked. This *pista* soon drops down towards the river again. On the right, marks lead up through the trees to follow a wide grassy trail which turns down to the river, following it N along its left bank. At the Barranco de Besiberri turn right to a small footbridge, a short way up E, that allows a crossing. Go down across rough pastures on the other side, NW then N, to pick up a *pista* going N. Pass a branch going to the camping area to the left across the river and the large Conangles hut, now an education centre. The *pista* continues, N, above the hut. Avoid the turning left to the Barcelona University Refugio. The *pista* becomes grassy as it winds towards the mouth of the Viella tunnel. There is a new tunnel under construction (July 2003) that has obliterated the GR11 route to the *refugio*. The new tunnel passes directly underneath the *refugio* and it seems that the best way to reach it is to walk a short distance along the old tunnel road to gain the *pista* to…

7.45 Hospital de Viella, 1630m. *Full refugio services at Refugi Sant Nicolau, including telephone. Bus service to Val d'Aran/Lleida at tunnel mouth.*

DAY 23
Hospital de Viella – Refugio de la Restanca

Maps: Editorial Alpina Ribagorça, and Val d'Aran. IGN Carte de randonnées Couserans. ICC No 5, Alta Ribagorça. Prames maps (1:40,000 and 1:50,000) 24.

Distance:	10.5km (7.1 miles)
Height gain:	770m
Height loss:	390m
Time:	4hrs 10mins

This is an easier day through the Conangles valley and up the delightful gully with cascading water to gain the final zigzags to Port de Rius. It is a popular family trip in the summer, with vehicle access so near. The route continues by boulder edged lakes to the head of the Arties valley at the eastern end of Estany de Rius, often only partly filled with its blue, copper-sulphate-looking water. However, fresh water is available a few hundred metres down the track at a small water pipe on the right. Then the route continues easily down the Arties valley, with one short, steep wooded ridge to surmount to the hut. The HRP route via Estany del Mar is an exquisite walk and well worth mentioning as an alternative. It is possible to walk the next three days in two, especially if camping.

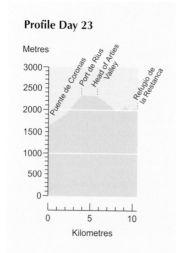

Profile Day 23

0.00 Hospital de Viella, 1630m. *The High Level Route joins from the west.* Take the track E between meadows above the Barranco de Hospital down on the right. This leads to a rocky *pista*, which is followed for about 300m until a grassy track can be taken to the left, just before the *pista* goes down to cross the stream. The track goes E, crosses the Barranc del Redó (Barranco de la Escaleta) and continues through trees then rough grazing with many boulders. It climbs NE to gain a gully, not easily seen from below, with a distinct path climbing N on its left side. Near the top the path crosses to its right side and then it is necessary to watch for an ascending path to the right. Straight on goes to Estany Redó, popular with fishermen. Take the path to the right, which climbs steeply NE to the narrow pass of...

1.45 Port de Rius, 2355m. *Tuc de l'Estany Redó lies to the NNW and Pic de Conangles to the SE.* Continue NE with a small lake to the right and then pass Estany de Rius by its north shore to reach at the eastern end...

2.15 Head of Arties valley (Barranco de Rius), 2340m. *The HRP goes south by the Estany Tort de Rius and Estany del Mar, a highly recommended alternative route to La Restanca.* Go down ESE along the right of the valley. The streambed to the left is usually dry at first. In

Camping: There are camping possibilities in the lower part of the Conangles valley and also in the valley to the west, the Mulleres valley. There is also a place by Estany Redó, just off the route. Also available just below the water pipe in the Arties valley and then many places below.

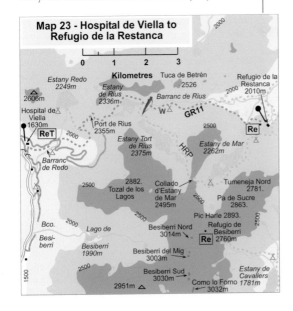

Map 23 - Hospital de Viella to Refugio de la Restanca

Estany de la Restanca

about 400m the small water point is found coming from the rock to the right of the path. A little lower, the first camping spot presents itself with water only suitable for washing. Drinking water must be collected from the pipe above. Continue down the right of the valley for another 2km or so, until a stony path to the right ESE can be taken. This climbs up and down along the side of the valley, over a small ridge and, turning into a side valley SE, crosses a stream. It then climbs very steeply through trees to a boggy place before going down past the old hut and so on to the dam and the new…

4.10 Refugio de la Restanca, 2010m. *About 80 places. Food and drinks service in the summer.*

DAY 24
Ref. de la Restanca – Ref. de Colomers

Distance:	7.5km (4.7 miles)
Height gain:	660m
Height loss:	555m
Time:	3hrs 40mins

Maps: Editorial Alpina Montardo. IGN Carte de randonnées Couserans. ICC No 5, Alta Ribagorça. Prames maps (1:40,000 and 1:50,000) 24.

Another shortish day with plenty of time to enjoy the scenery. The walk down from the Port de Caldes is easy, but the rest is rugged and quite hard. To describe the next two days as passing through the Spanish Pyrenean equivalent of the Lake District would not be amiss. A glance at the map shows seemingly countless lakes and tarns begging to be explored. Most of the summits rising from this watery landscape are quite accessible to walkers and there are places to camp almost at will. There are two routes to the Colomers hut. One goes NE down the Arties valley to turn SE to gain the Coll de Ribereta and then the hut. It is long and mostly over *pista*. The shorter and more delectable is described here.

0.00 Refugio de la Restanca, 2010m. From the *refugio* go SE steeply up the right-hand bank of the stream to pass the Estany Cap de Port on the right. From the far end climb very steeply to the south shoulder of Montardo d'Aran and the...
1.30 Port de Güellicrestada, 2475m. *National park boundary sign.* Go down E slightly to cross a stream coming from the south side of Montardo. *From here a trail rises N, without difficulty, to the summit. Estany Monges can be seen below to the right. A path S leads to the Refugio Ventosa i Calvell below the*

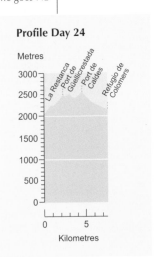

Profile Day 24

Camping: There is a grassy shelf above the Restanca to the SW towards Estany de Mar. If a visit to the Colomers hut is not required, then it is possible to contour, with some small ascents, ESE from Estany Mort to Estany Obago, with many lovely spots en route, though this is not quicker.

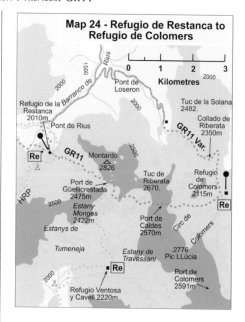

Map 24 - Refugio de Restanca to Refugio de Colomers

Agullas de Travessani. Continue ESE to an obvious small pass ahead on a SW branch off the SE ridge from the summit, following the left bank of the small stream issuing from it. *From this small pass can be seen the Port de Caldes towards the east, the Estanys of the same name below to the left, and to the right the large lake of Mengades.* Go down steeply to pass between the two upper lakes and then climb ESE to join the another path, coming up from the Ventosa hut, which is followed E to the...

2.30 Port de Caldes, 2570m. Go E past the small Cap de Rencules lake to the left and then go down to the valley E by large zigzags. Follow the path down the left of the stream to a small level grassy area where the other route joins from the left. Continue a short distance NE to...

3.40 Refugio de Colomers, 2115m. *Meals service in*

*Waterfall, Circ de Colomers
(day 24)*

Estany Gargulles in the Circ de Colomers

the season; some 30 places. When closed, the bothy Colomers 1 is open some 50m to the SSW.

DAY 25
Refugio de Colomers – Espot

Distance:	19.5km (12.1 miles)
Height gain:	500m
Height loss:	1295m
Time:	6hrs

Maps: Editorial Alpina Montardo and San Maurici. IGN Carte de randonnées Couserans. ICC No 5, Alta Ribagorça and ICC No 26, Pallars Sobirá. Prames maps (1:40,000 and 1:50,000) 25 and 26.

Back to longer distance walking, today the route climbs to the passes of Port de Ratera de Colomers and Port de Ratera d'Espot through delightful rugged mountain scenery and many lakes of the National Park of Aigüestortes and Sant Maurici. It descends through the Ratera valley, which is not much used now as most of the traffic goes via the Amitges refuge. It then goes past the lower Ratera lake and through the woods to the lake of Sant Maurici and along its shores before the equally

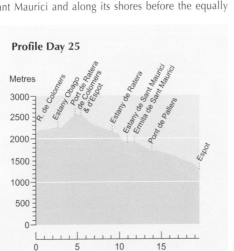

Profile Day 25

Camping: An overnight stop would be possible only to the west of Estany Obago and its environs, though even this may be illegal now. The campsites at Espot would be the next location.

delightful walk down to Espot, with even the short road sections not detracting from the sylvan experience. There are major changes afoot on the Espot side of the national park. The former car parking area at the eastern end of Lago Sant Maurici has been bulldozed and landscaped. No private vehicles are now allowed to the lake, and restricted access has been in force for a some time. A new parking area and barrier, near to the park boundary some 4km down the valley, has been constructed, with the idea that vehicle access will be permitted only to this point. Local Landrover taxis will be permitted to transport people to the lake, but only all the way from Espot. The first road section can be avoided by using an engineered footpath to the right.

0.00 Refugio de Colomers, 2115m. From the refuge cross the dam and go down to the left by some rail tracks to pick up the path going E up to a small pass and turning SE to go down to Estany Long (Llarg), passing its SW side. Continue SE along the SW side of the small Estany Redó and the stream to...

Pic de Crabes

0.50 Estany Obago, 2236m. This is also passed on its SW side. **Ignore any waymarks going straight on.** Turning left round the head of the lake the route crosses a stream and climbs E, then SE, with the mass of Pic de Ratera to the right, to reach the....

1.50 Port de Ratera de Colomers, 2580m. Continue across the pass, SE then ESE, past a small pool on the left, to reach...

2.00 Port de Ratera d'Espot, 2534m. *Please note that the IGN 1:50,000 map wrongly shows the route of the GR11 here. In the summer the Ratera valley will be most appreciated as it avoids the dust and Landrovers plying trade to the Amitges refuge. Remember, while in the national park waymarking will consist only of the occasional painted post or*

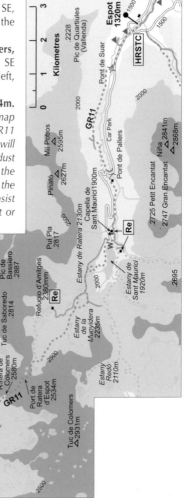

Map 25 - Refugio de Colomers to Espot

Estany de Sant Maurici

national park footpath sign (metal post with silhouette walker on attached plaque). Go down SE passing above and to the left of the Estany del Port de Ratera. The path climbing straight ahead, E, goes to the Amitges refuge, but be careful to find the track going down into the Ratera valley S to SE with occasional post markers. The path goes down the left side of the stream, passing to the left of the Estany de la Munyidera, eventually into pines and comes out onto a *pista*. It is important here to be certain where on this *pista* you have arrived. If on the last part of the track you maintained the left side, 40m down the *pista* to the right is a signpost. If, however, you find yourself across the stream it will be necessary to turn left on the *pista* to find the signpost at a Y-junction of *pistas*. If it isn't clear, **go downwards**, as both branches going westwards go uphill. Go down the *pista* ESE to…

3.10 Estany de Ratera, 2130m. Follow the *pista* down, SE, until, a short distance after it has crossed the stream, the Río Ratera, look out for a track going off right, SW, with a pole marker a short distance away. Take this trail, which passes the Cascade below by zigzags and then goes down to the Sant Maurici lake, where it turns along the north shore and continues to the end by the dam of…

4.00 Estany de Sant Maurici, 1920m. *Spring and information boards on the left; obelisk on right. The pista on
the right goes down to the Refugio Ernest Mallafré, 36
places, not always open outside of the holidays. Taxis to
Espot may be available from here.* Turn slightly right, S,
to follow the signposted *pista* going down E for about
70m and take the left branch down past a couple of
small zigzags with short-cuts to…

4.10 Capella de Sant Maurici, 1900m. *This is situated
beyond and immediately below the old car park, not as
on maps. There is a clean, usable bothy on the side of the
chapel with dual waterspouts below. Excellent place for a
lunch break or overnight stop.* Continue down the *pista*,
which shortly joins the road. A new, excellent path has
been engineered just to the right. Follow this to cross the
road just above the bridge called Pont de Pallers. Cross
the road and continue along the path until it turns down
to the right. Go straight on and up to join a grassy *pista*
with GR11 marks on a telegraph pole. Do not take the
pista ascending to the left, and in 2 or 3 minutes you
arrive at the national park green boundary fence and

*Monesterio valley,
near to Sant Maurici*

gate with GR11 post marker. Follow the main track beyond the gate, with occasional and comforting GR paint marks. The track eventually turns right down through old dry stone walls to the Pont de Suar wooden plank bridge over the stream and leads to a *pista* that climbs up to the road once more. *The old route through the fields is no longer in use.* Go down the road for 1km, passing Camping Vorla. A few minutes later you arrive at...

6.00 Espot, 1320m. *The GR11 access trail from Pont de Suert, via the Colomina hut, arrives at Espot from the south-west along the Peguera valley. Hotels, restaurants, bars, two shops for provisions and two campsites below the village. For lodgings see Jaume Vidal who runs the Bar Jouquim across the bridge. There is a very small campsite just below the road barrier across the bridge on the left and just before the village. For the nearest campsite below the village do not turn left across the bridge but go straight on between the buildings. Go over the Peguera stream and down the pista, where a back entrance to the site can be found on the GR11 route at the end of a small grassy meadow, with vehicle tracks indicating the way, just under 10mins from the village.*

DAY 26
Espot – La Guingueta

Distance:	9.5km (5.9 miles)
Height gain:	175m
Height loss:	550m
Time:	2hr 30mins

Maps: Editorial Alpina Sant Maurici, Pico d'Estats, and IGN Carte de randonnées Couserans. ICC No 26, Pallars Sobirá. Prames maps (1:40,000 and 1:50,000) 26.

Camping: Two campsites at La Guingueta

As Casa Pau at Estaon has closed, and the other accommodation is not always available, and because the only possibility of shelter beyond is at the Bordas de Nibrós, the day stage described in the previous edition has become impossibly long and so has been split into two. Also, the climb of well over 1200m, past Dorbé, can be very hard on a hot day. The once deserted *pista* to Jou has now been covered by tar-macadam and could be busy with day-trippers in the summer, but during the spring it still is a pleasant walk. Please note that the Editorial Alpina map shows a *pista* from Jou to La Guingueta, but this is not the case on the ground. Also, IGN 1:50,000 does not show the correct route of the GR11.

0.00 Espot, 1320m. From Espot keep to the right-hand bank of the River Escrita passing through the buildings to follow the *pista* down past the two campsites. Turn left down a steep *pista*, past the last site, crossing the Escrita and coming to the road where one turns left, going up for about 60m. Then turn right up the road to Estaís and Jou. Follow this road all the way to Jou without going up the turning to Estaís. **1.50 Jou, 1306m.** There is water at Jou, either from the stream just before the village or from the spring at the trough,

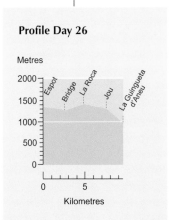

Profile Day 26

Map 26 - Espot to La Guingueta

Pic de Quartiules (Vallenda) .2228

1306m Jou W

La Guingueta 945m

HRS TC

Espot 1320m

HRSTC

Estais 1400m

Riu Escrita

GR11

Super Espot 1490m

Pui Alt .1826

Pui de Finistrelles 2027

0 1 2 3

Kilometres

Jou

which is found by taking the first concrete ramp straight ahead as one arrives at the buildings. In springtime the Vallenda and Lledeto streams also should be flowing. Once almost derelict, Jou now is being restored by new occupiers to life again. Follow the road through the bottom part of the village and take the signposted path down towards the Noguera Pallaresa valley on the right. Near the bottom, pass by a barn then through some inhabited buildings, taking the left branch of the road down into the village of…

2.30 La Guingueta d'Aneu, 945m. *Hotels with restaurant/bars, and two campsites – one with shop for provisions. Some mountain equipment, including boots, can be obtained in Esterri d'Aneu, 4km to the N.*

La Guingueta

DAY 27
La Guingueta – Bordas de Nibrós

Maps: Editorial Alpina Sant Maurici, Pico d'Estats, and IGN Carte de randonnées Couserans. ICC No 26, Pallars Sobirá. Prames maps (1:40,000 and 1:50,000) 29.

Camping: Wild camping only possible beyond Estaon.

Distance:	14.5km (9.0 miles)
Height gain:	1565m
Height loss:	1030m
Time:	6hrs 50mins

This is a hard day, and it is especially important to start early if the weather is likely to be hot. If it is hot, then this could prove to be the most demanding day of the whole route. It is well marked, with the exception of the section to the ridge above Dorbé.

0.00 La Guingueta d'Aneu, 945m. Take the signposted 'Dorbé' *pista* E, just to the left of the water point Font de Cyrille. Turn right, S, on the other side of the Embalse de Torrassa. Very shortly take the obvious path ascending

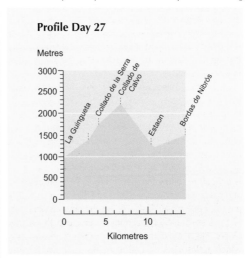

Profile Day 27

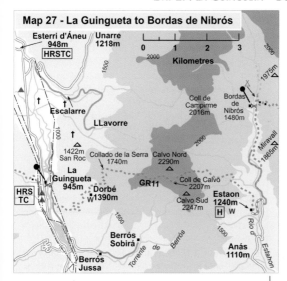

Map 27 - La Guingueta to Bordas de Nibrós

obliquely to the left with waymarks appearing a little later. Cross the fence and take the left branch, SE, following the waymarked track, which makes a large zigzag to the west, some 15–20mins below the village. On the final approach to the village follow waymarks either through the meadow on the left or take the track, if clear of brambles, to...

1.20 Dorbé, 1390m. *There is still one family living here, and has done so for at least 15 years, to my knowledge. In the square there is an important water point, as no water will be found until well after the high pass.* Go between the buildings above the water point and turn right. Pass through the village and turn left N across two fields and then NW up a small rocky ridge. From here it is difficult to follow the waymarks as there are old ones and new ones all over the place and then none at all. The pass that you are aiming for is not the obvious one to the N, but a small cleft that cannot be seen, exactly NE from Dorvé. High up NE there are two small clumps of birch which act as markers. Follow marks up the valley until large zigzags climb to the birch trees. These zigzags are not very clear as bikers have cut a more direct route. *Do spare some time to look back to see the view into the Noguera Pallaresa unfolding as height is gained.* Make your own way then to find the track way up above, which gives easy access through the thickening undergrowth to the narrow pass of...

2.35 Collado de la Serra, 1740m. Turn right, E, and follow the delightfully clear path climbing easily through the wood on the north side of the ridge. *This is the northern spur of the west ridge from Calvo north.* About 30mins later, go SE up through some small meadows and then 10–15mins later, at an old water trough, climb E by zigzags then S to the crest of the ridge. Turn left, NE, to follow the ridge for a while before turning across the head of the valley on the right above Berrós Sobirà, seen way below, to leave the trees and reach...

4.00 Coll de Calvo, 2207m. *Splendid view into the national park to the west. The path N goes to the obvious north summit of Calvo.* Go N for a few metres before turning down NE and then E. The route is quite easy to follow, but it is important to locate waymarks after it becomes vague over grassy patches. Follow the marks down which turn S towards an old telegraph pole, and just before reaching this the trail goes SE to another tall pole with waymarks. A few minutes later turn E again at a small meadow to go down the ridge past a signpost to Dorbé. A few more minutes later, well before the bottom of the ridge, look out for a path to the right going SSE, which turns SW into a small valley, turning SE after it crosses the stream. Follow the clear path SE then S to zigzag down the steep rocks to...

5.40 Estaon, 1240m. *Casa Pau, at the bottom of the rocks, no longer provides accommodation and meals. However, Snra Rosa Feliu Torrent, C. Cabalé, tel. 973 623 031, can accommodate four people, B&B plus evening meal for 30 Euros per person. This accommodation is not available for the first two weeks in August each year. The house is situated beside the GR11, about 20m before the road, with a water trough attached to the lower wall.*

There are several water points, the lowest being perhaps the best quality. For camping it would be necessary to go down to the stream and a short way into next day's stage. As this is a farming area, sufficient good water from Estaon should be carried. Water from the Ribera d'Estaon will need sterilising.

From Casa Pau pass down the narrow passageway to the road below. Signpost to La Guingueta and Dorbé. Turn left, E, and follow the road down, turning NNE, to the Río d'Estahon. Cross the bridge and immediately climb up the earth bank to the left to reach a *pista* in a few metres. Turn left, N, and follow the *pista* along the left bank. Some 10–15mins later, at another bridge, the route goes straight on along an old path. However, after crossing the bridge and re-crossing the river again a little later the *pista* becomes a path across a field to join with the old route once more. The *pista* way is preferable in wet weather. Continue N along the path passing…

6.50 Bordas de Nibrós, 1480m. *There is at least one building that can be used for an overnight stop. The best place for a camp would be a little further on, keeping to the true left bank.*

DAY 28
Bordas de Nibrós – Tavascan

Maps: Editorial Alpina Pica d'Estats. IGN Carte de randonnées Couserans. ICC No 26, Pallars Sobirá. Prames maps (1:40,000 and 1:50,000) 30.

Camping: Wild camping beside Lleret

Distance:	8.5km (5.3 miles)
Height gain:	400m
Height loss:	760m
Time:	3hrs 20mins

A much easier pastoral day past ancient, remote farm buildings then rising steeply to the Coll de Lleret, with the trail climbing to the top of the first crags beyond the village of Lleret, where there is accommodation and camping allowed. It follows an ancient track high above the valley of Noguera de Lladorre, sometimes crossing crags by dry stone engineering (care needed in places) before coming down to Aineto and Tavascan. There should be no problem with navigation.

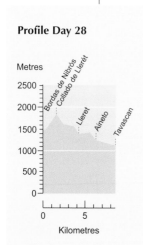

Profile Day 28

0.00 Bordas de Nibrós, 1480m. Continue N along the track but keep an eye out for the sharp turn back right, S, in about 3mins. Climb steeply up this path past a *borda* and then turn NE to reach another. Follow the marks around the left of this, taking the left branch, E, of the path beyond. About 10mins later the path turns sharp left, N, for a while before turning SE to reach the pass…

1.00 Coll de Llerét, 1830m. Go a few metres NE, then a few more SSE and then, after a few more, turn down E to reach in 10mins a signpost 'Estaon–Tavascan'. The marks lead SSE to a rough *pista* and zigzag down, eventually turning N to reach more turns E to the NW edge of…

1.55 Llerét, 1381m. *Villagers helpful and camping possible.* Continue NNE to the stream, a short way from the village. Then

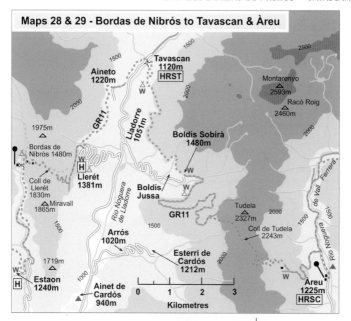

Maps 28 & 29 - Bordas de Nibrós to Tavascan & Àreu

turn left NNW up a path to cross the stream, continuing N on the other side to climb to the top of the first crags. Once located, the trail more or less contours high up the side of the valley. Much later, just before Aineto, it drops down ENE very steeply and it is necessary to follow the waymarks closely to reach the *pista* going S then N at the entrance to the village of…

3.05 Aineto, 1220m. Go up the steep concrete road to the left, N, which turns E around the top of the village. Look out for the wide track-cum-*pista* to the left, N. Take this all the way to…

3.20 Tavascan, 1120m. *A small village with hotels, restaurants, bars, shop and telephone. Both food and small equipment shops will open upon request.*

Refugio de Estós (Day 20)

DAY 29
Tavascan – Àreu

Maps: Editorial Alpina Pica d'Estats. IGN Carte de randonnées Couserans. ICC No 26, Pallars Sobirà. Prames maps (1:40,000 and 1:50,000) 30.

Camping: Campsite at Àreu, open during the summer only. Possible at *fuente* above Tavasacan and just beyond Boldís Sobirà.

Distance:	17.5km (10.9 miles)
Height gain:	1120m
Height loss:	1015m
Time:	6hrs 20mins

A steep haul through the woods above Tavascan leads to another high, contouring path down the Noguera Lladorre valley. Then there is a long *pista* climb through more woods to gain access to the Esterri de Cardós valley with the pass at its head. The route then goes steeply down to the *pista* above Àreu.

0.00 Tavascan, 1120m. Cross the bridge over the Río Noguera Lladorre, turning left to find immediately a waymarked track, on the right, climbing steeply up the line of a covered water channel. This crosses a *pista* and

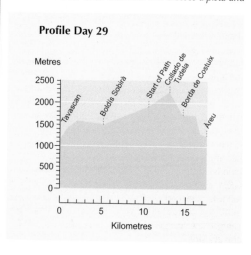

Profile Day 29

continues steeply to a small building to do with water supply. Turn right, S, crossing the *pista* again and climb steeply through the birch wood. After some time the gradient eases and the route comes to a small meadow, which is passed on the left. This leads to another field, which is also passed up on the left. The marks come to a *fuente* sign at a stone wall with a third grassy area above. *Possibility of a camp here.* Climb up through the trees on the left of this third meadow. Turn right, S, and follow this trail as it climbs to gain sufficient height to cross the side valley ahead above its steepest part. If the marks are lost, just keep climbing diagonally through the wood. Just before the gully take a right fork in the trail. Follow the clear path to the first fields above Boldís Sobirà, where it becomes indistinct for a short distance. Here, go straight on, close to the stone wall on the left, and the way becomes clear again. Follow the path down to…

2.05 Boldís Subirà, 1480m. *Water point. Some 15mins into the next section, just after the pista on the left, which goes into the private property, look out for a water point on the right and place to camp.* From the northern part of the village take the *pista* E, which crosses the Torrente de San Miguel and climbs SW through the trees towards the Roc de Bataller on the large W ridge of Tudela. Much later it turns back to the E and again turns SW. It turns to the E again and goes round another bend. Now, look out for the waymarked track off right, S, which climbs towards the S ridge of Tudela. The trail goes to the pass between two small hills, with small fenced enclosure, at the…

4.20 Coll de Tudela, 2243m. Go down SE into the wood, where care should be taken to locate the waymarks as they zigzag down eastwards to reach the Bordas de Costuix, where the path passes between two buildings to become a *pista* (water point). Follow the *pista* down, SE then NE, through large bends to the road above Àreu. *GR11 signpost, Coll de Tudela–Tavascan.* Turn right, S, following the road to…

6.20 Àreu, 1225m. *Hotel, restaurant, shop and campsite. Cheaper Residencia-Casa de Pages (RCP) also available.*

Maps: Editorial
Alpina Pica d'Estats.
IGN Carte de
randonnées Haute-
Ariège Andorre. ICC
No 26, Pallars
Sobirà. Prames maps
(1:40,000 and
1:50,000) 31.

Distance:	15.5km (9.6 miles)
Height gain:	1350m
Height loss:	60m
Time:	5hrs 30mins

The crossing of the Port de Baiau, tomorrow, is a serious
undertaking in bad weather or poor snow conditions
early in the season. Normally the snow is good in the
spring, but the following warning is given here because,
should weather or snow conditions be poor, it is better to
wait for a few days in Àreu for the weather to improve
than high on the mountainside. The danger lies in
passing the two lakes on the Andorran side of the pass if
the snow is deep and rotten. It can partly cover the lakes,

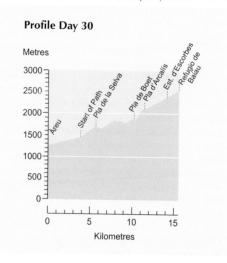

Profile Day 30

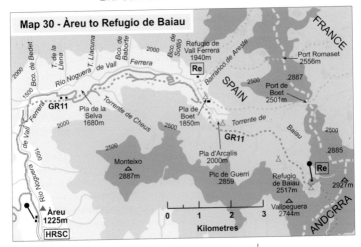

Map 30 - Àreu to Refugio de Baiau

masking the water's edge, and with the snow sloping steeply to the water, large blocks can break off into the lakes. Firm snow here is fine, but in soft, rotten conditions it becomes both difficult and dangerous. There are three ways of overcoming this problem if it is essential to continue into Andorra. Cross into Andorra by the HRP, which is lower than the GR11, via the pass to the north, Port de Boet, 2520m, with a brief passage down into France before ascending to cross the Port de Rat, 2542m, and into Andorra. Alternatively, use the Port de Romaset, 2556m, and continue on to Andorra by the Port de Creussans, 2622m. A third option, if the lake passage looks dicey, having crossed the Portella de Baiau, 2757m, is to avoid it by climbing SE along the rocky ridge to the north, starting at a small pass ENE from the Portella, which reaches the summit of Pic Alt de Coma Pedrosa, 2942m. An easy ridge to those used to scrambling (continental route grade 1). From the summit go down the S ridge to where one can either come off right across easy snow well above the lower lake or take the easy snow gully to the left and find the way down to the Coma Pedrosa. For today there are no

Camping: There are camping areas in the lower 'plas' and opportunities to camp higher until the grass runs out. It is also possible to camp beyond the Refugio de Baiau, beside the lake, just before the climb to the pass.

worries about snow or weather conditions, as the route passes through wooded valleys then climbs more steeply across open ground surrounded by high mountain wilderness. To the north lies the highest mountain in Cataluña, Pica d'Estats, 3143m, on a remote part of the border with France.

0.00 Àreu, 1225m. Leave the village by the road, N, which soon becomes a *pista* passing the left turn to the Coll de Tudela. In just under 3km turn right across the Rio Noguera de Vall Ferrera and continue N along the left bank for about 5mins before turning right, ENE, going up a path passing by stone walls and some *bordas* where the trail becomes grassy. It soon joins the main *pista*, which is crossed to take a steeply ascending track, which short-cuts a large loop to join the *pista* again just before...

1.40 Pla de la Selva, 1680m. *Camping no longer permitted.* Follow the left branch of the *pista* and some minutes later look out for a path right, E, going up into a pine plantation. Follow this and some time later it becomes a forest *pista*. Some 5–10mins later take an undulating path, right, which goes down to join the main *pista* from Àreu again. Cross the *pista* to a path at a right-hand bend, which allows a short-cut, joining the *pista* above, or one can just follow the *pista*. As the *pista* turns SE towards the Pla de Boet there is a sign on the left and...

2.55 Path to Refugio de Vall Ferrera, 1840m. *The hut (with guardian during the summer) lies 15–20mins to the north at 1940m. Take this path down to cross the stream for the Port de Boet route. Camping area in the Pla de Boet.* For the GR11, follow the *pista* SE above the Pla de Boet and in 10mins, where the *pista* turns sharp right, go straight on along a path SSE. The path climbs to another high pasture, the Pla d'Arcalís, where it passes close to the stream, still on the left bank. It then climbs E, crossing a side stream, and continues climbing ENE before turning SSE to reach...

4.55 Estany d'Ascorbes, 2360m. Pass the lakes on their E side passing through rocks and grass ESE then SSE,

turning E to cross the stream coming from the Estany de Baiau, and climb the steep rocky promontory to the hut...
5.30 Refugio de Baiau (J.M. Montfort), 2517m. *Metal hut perched on a promontory above the lake to the NW. In good condition, with kitchen area. Water from the lake.*

Andorran side of the Portella de Baiau (Day 31)

DAY 31
Refugio de Baiau – Arans

Maps: Editorial Alpina Andorra. IGN Carte de randonnées Haute Ariège Andorre. Prames maps (1:40,000 and 1:50,000) 32.

Camping: Ansalonga and Xixerella, with bar and restaurant (see above).

Distance:	15.0km (7.1 miles)
Height gain:	750m
Height loss:	1905m
Time:	6hrs 10mins

Today the route passes into Andorra. The following information is provided to assist in your plans. The route from Arinsal to Encamp involves some very steep ups and downs. From Encamp, to the east, the gradients ease. Beyond Coma Pedrosa wild camping is difficult due to lack of water or sites. There is one campsite near Arans, at Ansalonga, complete with shop. There is a spot just south of and above La Cortinada where one could pitch a tent, if the above campsite is closed. The tourist office

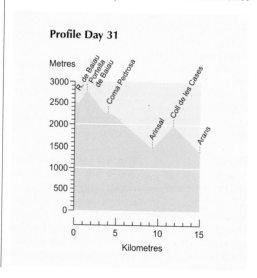

Profile Day 31

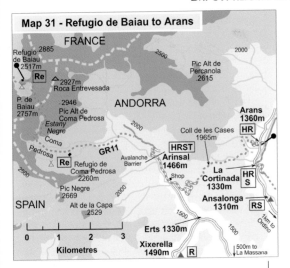

Map 31 - Refugio de Baiau to Arans

advises using the excellent site at Xixerella (pronounced chi-cher-ray-ya), 3.5km from Arinsal by road, SE down to Erts then right, SSW, up to the campsite, which is owned by a Cataluñan with British wife and staff. There is a bus service, but it is probably quicker to walk. There is also a bus service from Arinsal to La Massana, Ordino, Arans and down to Andorra la Viella. The route from La Cortinada to just above Ordino is pleasant enough, but involves 400m of steep ascent and descent, whereas the road route is much shorter and involves 60m down then up. There is a choice, then, of which way to go.

0.00 Refugio de Baiau, 2517m. From the hut go E down to the lake, continuing around the lake, cross a rock step and climb the first obvious grassy gully before turning SSE across the boulder field. Pick the best route to the steep loose section high above and then go ESE up the top very steep and loose scree section. Take care! You will probably find that the most worn part is the easiest. This brings you to the high pass and border with Andorra at the...

1.10 Portella de Baiau, 2757m. *From here, one of Andorra's many GR routes, the GR11-9A, follows the ridge to the right.* Go down easily SE then SSW to pass the upper lake, Estany Negre, on the left, E. Continue down, SSW, passing the lower lake on the left also. Cross the stream below, continuing down, S, to turn progressively E into the large hanging valley of Coma Pedrosa. *The refugio of the same name can be seen above the trail to the right beside Estany de los Truites.* Go down E to the mouth of the valley, passing a cabin over on the left suitable for an overnight stop. *From the mouth of the valley the Refugio de Coma Pedrosa, 2260m, lies above to the south.* Go down E into a small, delightful hollow to cross to the right of the stream coming from the Estany de los Truites. Follow the right of the stream down steeply into the wood. Much later the path turns N and comes to a junction of streams called the Aigües Juntes. These are crossed by two small footbridges. Follow the path on the other side generally E to reach a *pista* above, which is followed to the road. *There is a huge avalanche protection wall ahead, right across the valley.* Turn right

Pic Alt de Coma Pedrosa from Arinsal

following the road steeply down, turning SE to pass through the wall by a road and foot tunnel into...

4.00 Arinsal, 1466m. *Hotels, restaurants, and shop on the left just before the road to the left, Carretera Mas Ribafreta. This is the wide road that forks left near to the bottom of the town.* Turn left up this road, SE, and follow the road as it turns left, passing some flats before turning back SE again. A short time later take the path left, signposted 'Cami de Coll de les Cases', and if it is overgrown continue up the *pista* for 80m as it turns left to join with the path. Clear marks lead the way steeply up through the wood by zigzags, generally in a NNE direction, turning NE to the grassy pass of...

5.15 Coll de les Cases, 1965m. Go down NNE over grass to locate waymarks on trees that lead down a wooded gully ENE then ESE. After about 15–20mins, leave the gully, E then N, and a few minutes later it turns NW. Five minutes later leave a grassy track to the right, but go down left to cross a stream going up NE on the other side to cross another stream. A few more minutes later take a right turn, E, which leads to a *pista* going NNE. Follow this as it turns back S to join a road which winds its way down into...

6.10 Arans, 1360m. *Small hamlet with hotel, bar/restaurants, but no shop. It is about 3km south to the Ansalonga campsite.*

DAY 32
Arans – Encamp

Maps: Editorial Alpina Andorra. IGN Carte de randonnées Haute-Ariège Andorre. Prames maps (1:40,000 and 1:50,000) 32.

Camping: Campsite at Encamp. Possibility of camping just below the Coll d'Ordino in the early part of the season when water is present.

Distance:	14.5km (9.0 miles)
Height gain:	1010m
Height loss:	1090m
Time:	4hrs 45mins

The route follows the left of the Valira del Nord river, down to the next village, before climbing along the lower SW flank of Casamanya to overlook Ordino and then descending to within a short distance of it. (See introduction to yesterday's stage.) Then by a complex mix of *pista*s and paths, well marked and not difficult to follow, the route climbs to the Coll d'Ordino. It continues across grass and through woods to the very steep descent past terraces to the town of Encamp, seen and heard below.

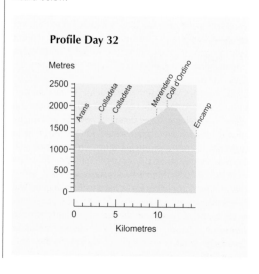

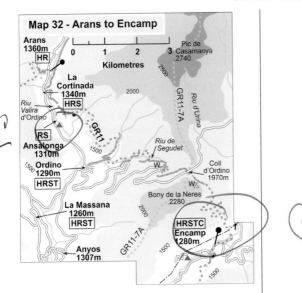

Map 32 - Arans to Encamp

Arans
1360m
HR

0   1   2   3
Kilometres

Pic de
Casamanya
.2740

La
Cortinada
1340m
HRS

2500

GR11-7A

Riu d'Urina

Riu
Valira
d'Ordino

2000

GR11

RS
Ansalonga
1310m

1500

Riu de
Segudet

Coll
d'Ordino
1970m

Ordino
1290m
HRST

W

1500

W

Bony de la Neres
.2280

La Massana
1260m
HRST

2000

HRSTC
Encamp
1280m

GR11-7A

1500

Anyos
1307m

1500

0.00 Arans, 1360m. Cross the road, E, and go down beside the restaurant La Font d'Arans to cross the river Valira del Nord. *The GR11-2A joins from the left.* Turn right, S, and go along the *pista*. About 10mins later, cross the bridge on the right to join the road, turning left down to…

0.15 La Cortinada, 1340m. *Hotel, bar/restaurant and shop.* Go E across another bridge to the old part of the village and follow narrow streets, SE, SW, SE and finally NE, to find a *pista* (probably a road now) going up SE to some houses. Go past the buildings, cross a chain and the *pista* becomes a path. *About 3mins later there is a small meadow above on the left suitable for a tent, with a stream 100m further on.* Cross the stream taking the left, S, fork which zigzags steeply up through the trees, later to contour past a farm on the right to another stream. From the second stream, about 40mins from La Cortinada, go up again steeply by zigzags, SE then SSE. About 30mins from the second stream, the trail turns sharp left, E, on the final climb. *Viewpoint overlooking Ordino.* In 15mins or so the trail arrives at a *pista*. Turn right and go steeply down, S then SW, turning sharply E. At the bottom, it turns to the W...

2.05 Junction to Ordino, 1360m. *The* pista *continues down to Ordino in about 10mins, where there are all the usual services, including a shop for provisions upon entering the town.* Now for the climb to the Coll d'Ordino. Take the ascending waymarked path E, ignoring a path climbing to the right, and in about 7mins it turns left across a stream, climbing NW to the top of the bank, then turns right, NE. Ten minutes later cross the stream to the right, turning left, E, up to a *pista*. Turn left, NE, along the *pista*, crossing the stream again, with the waymarks leading off the *pista* to a trail to the left, more or less parallel to it. The waymarked route crosses this *pista* to follow a path, which soon crosses a stream by a wooden bridge on the right, E, then turns left, N, for a few metres before turning back S and then E to climb beside another stream. Five minutes later it climbs to the terminus of a *pista*. Turn right, SW, and in a few minutes take the obvious steeply climbing *pista* to the left, SW turning E. This climbs to a picnic area beside the road in about 30mins. Shortly before the picnic area, take a left branch which climbs even more steepkly, with the gradient assuaged by a path which, within a few metres, turns off left, E, then turns back across the steep *pista* and then up E to...

3.10 Merendero, 1780m. *Water available but with limited flow.* Go up S by the path to the left of the wire-fenced compound to join an old *pista* climbing E. This *pista*, with a final bend to the SW, arrives at the road a few metres below...

3.35 Coll d'Ordino, 1970m. Cross the road and go up over grass to the high point and orientation table. Signpost 'Les Bons 1hr 30mins'. *The GR11-7A crosses here, climbing over the Pic de Casamanyá to gain the enticing ridges to the north. Another day perhaps!* Go down SE, just left of an obvious level path, to find a grassy *pista*, which is followed SE. It becomes indistinct as it crosses a boggy area (in springtime) where it is possible to camp if water is still flowing in the small stream. A clear path is followed as it enters the wood, SE. *(If you are following a route without waymarks, you are probably too high.)* This turns SW before turning slightly left to descend very steeply past terraced fields, generally SE. The route is well marked, leading ENE to a stream at one point. About 15mins later, as the path turns E again just before a building, look out for a turn right, S. Follow the path down, over the small rocky path, to the small Ermita de Sant Roma. Then go down to the road Carrer de Sant Roma and over the bridge Pont de les Bons. Turn right down the Avenida de Rouillac to...

4.45 Encamp, 1280m. *Fairly large town with all services and campsite. Continue down the main road SW about 600m, then turn right to the town park. Turn left, and about 150m from the park turn left into Camping International.*

Maps: Editorial
Alpina Andorra. IGN
Carte de randonnées
Haute-Ariège
Andorre. ICC No 15,
Cerdanya. Prames
maps (1:40,000 and
1:50,000) 33.

Distance:	20.5km (12.7 miles)
Height gain:	1350m
Height loss:	560m
Time:	6hrs

The Riu Madriu valley remains, for the present, the only main valley in Andorra not containing a road or *pista*. There are plans to change this state of affairs, but there is also a strong anti-road lobby from within Andorra. The road that has been laid from Les Escaldes to Estany d'Engolasters just passes the entrance, and only a few hundred metres are used by the GR11. The Madriu, though surrounded by high mountains, has a gentle ambience. Running water and many camping spots no doubt help. This really is a pleasant and civilised walk

Profile Day 33

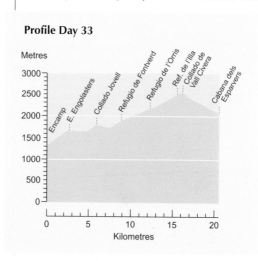

176

into walkers-only territory, with morning coffee at Estany d'Engo-lasters before the gentle walk over the small pass into the long, easy Madriu valley. Soon all the bustle of town and road is forgotten in this idyllic haven of peace and tranquillity, spoiled only by aggressive mosquitoes. The area is popular with walkers and fly fishermen.

Note: The tiny stone bothy at Epsarvers is really only suitable in an emergency. If you are without a tent, you could stop at L'Illa and then at Malniu.

0.00 Encamp, 1280m. From Camping International, turn right and right again, passing the park, to the main road. Turn left, and in about 150m cross the main road and take the road Carrer d'Engolasters that turns left round the building with an outside spiral concrete pedestrian way on its left. Follow it around to the left of

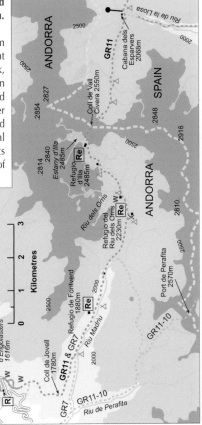

Map 33 - Encamp to Cabana del Esparvers

Camping: There are many places to camp in the Riu Madriu valley when the trail passes near to the river. On the other side of the pass one can camp below the first part of the descent and beyond the stone hut of Esparvers down by the stream.

the building to find a *pista* behind, Cami de l'Arena. Turn right, WSW, along the *pista*, ignore a grassy track left but take an ascending *pista* to the left, S, by a power line, about 4mins from the road. Three minutes later it becomes a path, W then SW. Some minutes later ignore a path to the left but carry straight on W with a short turn to the left, SE, before continuing generally SSW to the northern end of…

1.05 Estany d'Engolasters, 1616m. Cross the chain to new bar/restaurant above to the left. Take the *pista* around the SE side of the lake to the dam at the other end. Just after the dam take a path E, and in a few minutes it arrives at a car parking area and bar/restaurant at the end of the road which comes up from Les Escaldes. Go down the road, ENE, to the first sharp bend to the right. Ignore signs of a track to the left, NNE, but take the *pista* further round the bend, which leaves to the left, SE. Very soon this passes a *pista* to the right, then a water point. A few minutes later the *pista* divides. One way goes up left, over the small ridge ahead. Take the one going straight on through a small tunnel. Another water point is reached shortly, and soon after the *pista* becomes a path going SSE, soon to reach a picnic area and further water point. The trail is soon joined from the right by the GR11-12A and climbs the short distance to…

1.40 Coll de Jovell, 1780m. Cross the pass, SW, to pick up the path steeply descending to the ESE, which is joined at the bottom by the GR7 coming from the right, before climbing along the right of the Riu Madriu. Some time later take the left branch of the path SE. Still climbing, the trail passes through a gate and shortly arrives at…

2.30 Refugio de Fontverd, 1880m. *Good hut suitable for overnight stop; six places. Beware of especially aggressive mosquitoes at some of the obvious picnic spots by the river.* The track climbs clearly along the north side of the river, ESE, leaving it for a short while, SE, as the river makes a bend to the south. It joins the river again upon entering the high pasture, Pla de

Summer camp! Val d'Incles, on approach to Day 33

l'Ingla, with a small cabin to the right over a log bridge. Continue across the meadow climbing ENE and in a few minutes arrive at the…

3.45 Refugio del Riu dels Orris, 2230m. *Good hut with six places and spring a few metres away to the NW. Camping close by.* Follow the marks as they turn towards the NE, passing small lakes, more camping places and a hut after about 35mins. Ten minutes later cross a log bridge turning SE then NE again to reach…

4.40 Refugio de l'Illa, 2485m. *Large and now extended unmanned hut.* From the east of the hut take the ascending path to the large lake above. Take the right fork, E, to easily reach the…

4.55 Coll de Vall Civera, 2550m. Go SE down to the left bank of a stream. A little later the path crosses the stream and returns to the left bank, shortly turning E then SE towards the bottom of the valley. *The mountain ridge ahead is that enclosing the south side of Vall Civera, but as the trail turns to the E, tomorrow's route is seen ahead. It would be a good idea to make a mental note of its geography to aid navigation. The route will climb into the*

Portella de Calm Colomer from Coll de Vall Civera

hanging valley seen above the treeline, ESE, with the pass, just beyond the head of this valley, to the left. Keep to the right of a grassy ridge to pick up the trail a little lower. Follow this down to cross to the right-hand bank some time later. Take care now to keep an eye out for the point where the GR11 turns down left from the GR11–10. Waymarks and sign on the right. Cross the stream where possible (the footbridge has collapsed) and go up NNE to locate the small stone-built cabin...

6.00 Cabana dels Esparvers, 2068m. *Small stone cabin, looking like a grassy mound, with very narrow entrance; two or three places.* Take the ascending path E to find the descent to the river, reached in a few minutes, where one can camp.

DAY 34
Cabana dels
Esparvers – Refugio de Malniu

Distance:	10.3km (6.4 miles)
Height gain:	810m
Height loss:	740m
Time:	4hrs

Maps: Editorial Alpina Cerdanya. ICC No 15, Cerdanya. Prames maps (1:40,000 and 1:50,000) 35.

There is a steep climb today before the gradient eases to the Portella. There follows a very steep descent, then the route passes by lakes and through boulders and meadows – some care is needed to locate the Refugio Engorgs. With an early climb and then mostly downhill, it is quite easy to combine Days 34 and 35 if Camping Pirineus, below Seneja, is the target.

0.00 Cabana dels Esparvers, 2068m. *An old route used to go north from here before climbing back southwards to gain the hanging valley before the pass. Other waymarks can be found in the wood to the east. The better part of an afternoon was spent investigating the lower part of the ascent without being absolutely certain of the current way.* From the bothy, go up the grassy rise to the east to locate the path, with clear marks going down to and crossing the stream. Height has to be gained in the wood ahead. Marks leading farther north might lead back into this wood. However, go a few metres S by the left bank of the stream, turning SE to climb to a large grassy area. The clear path vanishes, but carry straight on SE across the grass,

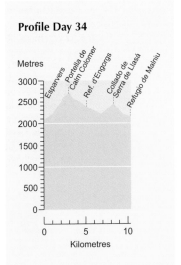

Profile Day 34

Camping: Places can be found by the lakes below the pass and in the small valley above and before the Refugio Engorgs. Camping is allowed at Malniu. It costs 2 Euros per person and the area is situated a few hundred metres before the *refugio*. Best to pitch first and pay later!

with the trees on the left, towards the trees on the other side. Keep a look out for a grassy ramp that climbs back, NNW, into the wood. Follow this until the gradient eases and further height can be gained by climbing tracks through the undergrowth. It winds its way upward in an easterly direction to a clear waymarked path above. The path goes SE and in a few minutes turns N to grass and then E to a cairned boulder. A few minutes later it climbs SE again, turning E into the hanging valley. The path crosses to the other side of the valley climbing its left side, ENE. Five minutes later the route turns sharply right, S, to reach the top of the valley side. Ignore a waymark on a large rock on the right but turn gradually left, ENE, to reach the obvious low saddle ahead...

1.30 Portella de Calm Colomer, 2680m. *Fine views. The other side is extremely steep. Remaining snow is also steep, and although fairly easy to climb in good condition it can be rather daunting to descend. It can be avoided by using rocks on the left. It is essential not to descend further from below these rocks, as the ground below is treacherous. Cross the slope beneath the snow*

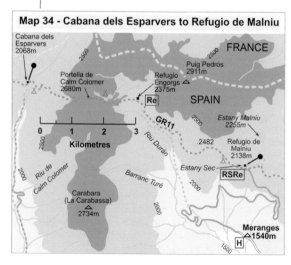

Map 34 - Cabana dels Esparvers to Refugio de Malniu

Looking back to Calm Colomer

to continue the descent over scree to the south and to where waymarks appear again. Without the hazard of snow, follow waymarks to the right, SE, which lead diagonally across the slope, passing over a small rocky ridge, before reaching easier ground. Continue SE until the route turns NE for a while, becoming unclear. Do not go straight on over the low ridge ahead but turn SSE around it; follow a faint path turning NE to arrive at the head of a small valley. Follow the valley down, E, to…

2.15 Refugio Engorgs, 2375m. *Hut in very good condition with table, fireplace and first aid kit. Room for 12–18 people. Water from the stream.* Go down SE to cross the Riu Duran, going S then SE, around the grassy area on the other side. Keep to the right and do not climb the steep edge but locate the steeply descending path. Shortly, take the left branch, SE. *The one on the right goes down to Meranges, where there is accommodation.* Ascend a little to pass the lower slopes of the SW ridge of Puig Pedros before continuing the descent SE. Cross various streams, at one boggy place by a fallen tree, and

Refugio Engorgs

climb to the left to find the trail, which climbs S then E to a Collado on the ridge called Serra de Llasa. Go down, NE then E past the camping area. Leave the trees behind, with the picnic area below in view. Go down the fields to a wooden bridge crossing the stream coming from the Estany Sec, which leads to the car parking area and...

4.00 Refugio de Malniu, 2138m. *Large hut with guardian during the summer, accommodating 40; bar and small shop available at this time for expensive refreshments and provisions. Due to access by pista, this is very busy during the holiday period with such delightful scenery to the north. Camping nearby.*

DAY 35
Refugio de Malniu – Puigcerdà

Distance:	15km (9.3 miles)
Height gain:	95m
Height loss:	1030m
Time:	3hrs 20mins

Maps: Editorial Alpina Cerdanya. ICC No 15, Cerdanya. Prames maps (1:40,000 and 1:50,000) 36.

The GR11 makes its way down from the mountains to the high plateau area around Puigcerdà. The route is fairly well marked, though some care is needed in the grassy places and at the start. This is an easy day, swinging down paths and *pista*s.

0.00 Refugio de Malniu, 2138m. Go down across the *pista*-bridge turning left, E, along an old trail, which climbs through the wood towards the Estany Malniu. Seven minutes later take the right branch, E, and then in a couple of minutes ignore the waymarks, continuing

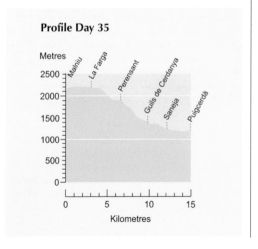

Profile Day 35

Camping: Camping Pirineus, just beyond Seneja, does not open until the end of June. The campsite beyond Puigcerdà should be open all year. It would be possible to camp near the water canal just before point 1750 and 50m beyond Refugio de Feixa. Puigcerdà provides the only other accommodation.

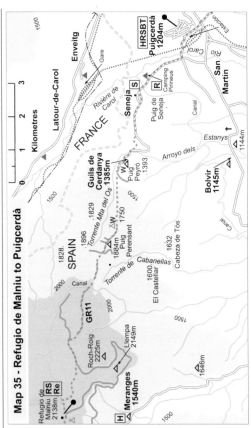

straight on to the lake, but look out for a turning to the right climbing S, also through the trees, but not so clearly marked. The trail turns to the E, losing a little height. It goes across a stream and passes a pond to the left. When a rough *pista* comes from the right, keep on SE a few metres to another *pista*, then E across an open grassy area with the line of a large *pista* seen to the right. Continue E to join the main *pista* and follow it NE to within sight of the Refugio de Feixa over on the left.

There is a good water source 50m beyond the refugio, on the northern side of the pista. Before reaching the *refugio*, keep a look out for marks indicating the place to turn right across grass to soon pick up a grassy *pista* going SE. Continue along this *pista,* which turns E, and ignore a branch to the left. Four minutes later it becomes indistinct across grass, but continue SE and in 5mins the *pista* is clear again, going ESE and soon turning E. It becomes unclear again at another grassy place where, ignoring a waymark on the right, you follow vehicle tracks to the left which turn SE. Go across the main *pista* ahead. *This is the one that comes from Malniu past the Refugio de Feixa.* Go across grass, ESE, to find the *pista* going down into the wood. Pass two *pistas* to the left a few minutes later, and in a few more minutes pass through a fence and on down to an open grassy area. Cross a small stream issuing from the small canal on the left and go up the ridge E, passing a rocky outcrop on the left, though either side will do. Continue steeply down the ridge, E, by a stony gully. Much later, as the path becomes indistinct over grass, ignore a farm *pista* slightly below to the right, but continue straight on, slightly north of east, to cross a stream. Continue E and down to the *pista* on the left below. This becomes a road. Soon take the left fork, which turns to the right, and a little later turn left to the main square of…

2.05 Guils de Cerdanya, 1385m. *Water point in main square and newly opened bar/restaurant.* Take the SE exit from the square down to the main road. Go along the road about 300m and where it bends to the right carry straight on along a *pista*, SE. At the junction ahead turn right, SSE, down to the road again. Turn left, E, and follow all the way to…

2.35 Seneja, 1220m. *Small shop behind the church.* Pass through the village on to the main road again, passing Camping Pirineus over on the left. *When open, this site has a bar/restaurant and shop.* Follow the main road SE to cross, E, the large bridge over the Río Carol. The road winds its way to the SE again, passing a bar/restaurant.

Puigcerdà

Continue along the road SE to the railway station square where steps to the left, NE, climb to...

3.20 Puigcerdà, 1204m. *All services are to be found here. If the town is not required, continue SE from the station to the main road and the turning to Age.*

DAY 36
Puigcerdà – Planoles

Distance:	26.5km (16.5 miles)
Height gain:	1020m
Height loss:	1085m
Time:	7hrs

Maps: Editorial Alpina Cerdanya. ICC Nos 15 & 31, Cerdanya and Ripolles. Prames maps (1:40,000 and 1:50,000) 37.

This is a long day. The only real possibility of making it shorter is to camp in a meadow just before the Torrente de Punt Turo above Dórria. The route uses the road to just beyond Vilallobent and then climbs to a little pass to gain entry to a narrow valley, which is ascended along its right-hand bank, eventually reaching the floor of the valley. A *pista* is then followed for a while before turning to climb to the border and then following the long descent by *pista* to Dórria and an old trail to Planoles. Waymarking is not all that it should be, and it can be confusing on the border ridge in cloud. It is

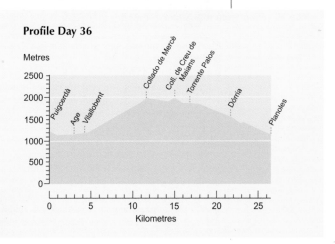

Profile Day 36

Metres

2500
2000
1500
1000
500
0

Puigcerdà · Age · Vilallobent · Collado de Mercè · Coll. de Creu de Maians · Torrente Palos · Dórria · Planoles

0   5   10   15   20   25

Kilometres

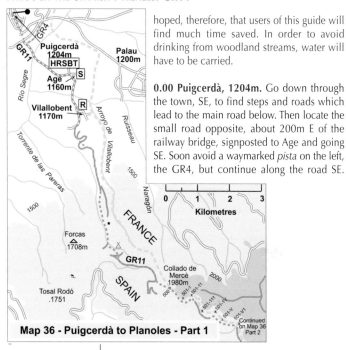

Map 36 - Puigcerdà to Planoles - Part 1

hoped, therefore, that users of this guide will find much time saved. In order to avoid drinking from woodland streams, water will have to be carried.

0.00 Puigcerdà, 1204m. Go down through the town, SE, to find steps and roads which lead to the main road below. Then locate the small road opposite, about 200m E of the railway bridge, signposted to Age and going SE. Soon avoid a waymarked *pista* on the left, the GR4, but continue along the road SE.

Climb steeply through Age, where there is a shop. Pass by the turning left to...

0.45 Vilallobent, 1170m. *There is a bar/restaurant here.* A few minutes S along a cement road, take the unlikely very steep earth *pista* (very muddy when wet) that climbs SW, turning S then E. A few minutes after it has turned E, keep a look out for a path to the right. Take the path ESE, which turns S to soon arrive at the *pista* again. Turn right and soon left onto a path that arrives at a small pass and *pista*. Turn left, E, and follow the *pista* as it turns S, climbing the right of the tree-filled valley. The *pista* has been extended, so after about 20mins look out for a track going straight on, as the *pista* turns to the left. Follow the path S, avoiding a grassy *pista* to the right. A few minutes later avoid a path to the right but go on S, turning SE then

S again soon to reach a large *pista*. Cross the *pista* to pick up one beyond travelling SE. Follow this for about 2km before, at a right bend, going up steeply left, SE. Bear left slightly towards the top to reach the border with France and border stone (BS) No.500 at…

3.00 Collado de Mercè, 1980m. *In fact the border fence and ditch do not follow the line of the border stones here. The border marked on maps follows the border stones. However, the frontier ditch and fence lie further up the slope to the NE. So, in cloud, if the way is not known, and not grasped from the maps, there can be considerable confusion, especially after BS 501-II. In misty conditions, from BS 500 go ESE across grass just below the high ground with BS 501-I below to the right. This bearing should bring you to the fence, ditch and cattle grid gate in the fence by BS 501-II in less than 10mins. On a clear day follow the path SE from BS 500, then NE to the same point.* Do not follow the obvious path SE into the trees below the fence but go across the grass, SE, below the trees to locate a waymark on a boulder. This is visible only when standing to the south side of the BS 501-II, as the rock is mostly hidden by a bush. A waymarked *pista* soon appears which is followed

Camping: There are no campsites, but a good place can be found in the meadow just beside the Torrente de Punt Turo. It might also be possible to find a spot in the wood where the trail crosses the small stream below the house marked on the sketch map. There is another possible place where the *pista* crosses the Torrente Palos. There is a campsite above Planoles.

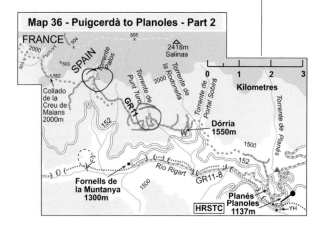

Map 36 - Puigcerdà to Planoles - Part 2

FRANCE

SPAIN

2418m Salinas

Collado de la Creu de Maians 2000m

Dórria 1550m

GR11

Torrente Palos

Torrente de Punt Turo

Torrente de la Rodonella

Torrente de Portal Sobirà

Torrente de Planés

0   1   2   3
Kilometres

1500

Río Rigart

GR11-8

152

Fornells de la Muntanya 1300m

Planés Planoles 1137m

HRSTC

YH

down SE into the trees past BS 501-III. The *pista* soon becomes a path, passing BS 501-IV and 501-V, and at 501-VI a new *pista*, which has mostly obliterated the old path, is climbed steeply S to reach BS 502. Cross the fence line ahead, with memorial cross on the right…

3.50 Collado de la Creu de Maians, 2000m. *There is no longer a clear way down from here and all guides are vague. It is necessary to descend slightly south of east to cut a pista about 100m below and about 700m distant.* Go down E across grass to the obvious hollow, which becomes a narrow grassy gully where a way-mark can be located. From this mark either take the track going into the wood, E, and find easy ways down through the trees, without difficulties, always on an E bearing, until the *pista* is reached, or try following the gully, which I am informed is the proper route. Turn left, NE, following the *pista* to cross the Torrente de Palos, turning then SE. A waymarked path is followed now, below and instead of the *pista*, and about 50mins later the Torrente de Punt Turo is reached. *Camping spot just above the pista to the left, before the stream.* Continue along the *pista* SE, which turns to the N then S before coming to the road below…

5.35 Dórria, 1550m. *The GR11-8 continues straight on down the road and might be considered as an alternative if this already long day is being split. The next section of the GR11 is overgrown with occasional thorns and brambles and needs clearing. It is quite manageable in dry conditions, but in the wet it is very unpleasant, and either the GR11-8 or the main road would be a good choice, though both of these add over 2km.* The GR11 turns sharp left, N, down a *pista* to the stream below. Cross the stream and continue on to another, the Torrente de Portal Sobirà, which is very slippery. **Take care!** Follow the old trail first SSE then turning E to cross a small pass before continuing down SE then E. With joy, it becomes a *pista,* and in a few minutes turn right steeply down S, with the *pista* becoming a cement road joining the main road. Cross the road beside the Hostal de la Carretera and go down S though Planés. If going

The Youth Hostel, Planoles

directly to the youth hostel, take the path and steps on the right as the road turns to go down N. Otherwise, follow the road down to the river then E across the bridge and up steeply, ENE, into...

7.00 Planoles, 1137m. *Youth hostel and bar/restaurant near the railway station below the town. Bar/restaurant, B&B and shops for provisions in the upper town. The campsite Can Fosset is above the town beside tomorrow's route.*

DAY 37
Planoles – Núria

Maps: Editorial Alpina Cerdanya and Puigmal. ICC Nos 31 & 2, Ripolles and Alt Empordá. Prames maps (1:40,000 and 1:50,000) 38.

Distance:	21km (13.1 miles)
Height gain:	1600m
Height loss:	770m
Time:	6hrs 30mins

This day involves quite a bit of ascent. However, it could be split by staying at Queralbs or by camping above Dórria during the previous day and by using the camping spot during this day. The climb from Planoles is pleasant enough, though hard when off-road. All in all, a varied and pleasing walk, culminating in the climb along the spectacular Río Núria gorge.

0.00 Planoles, 1137m. *There are two cement roads going north from the main road above the town. The GR11 takes the westerly one. The tarmac road curving*

Profile Day 37

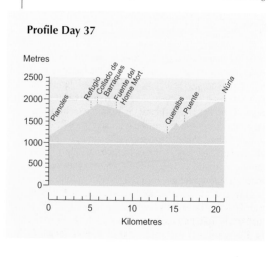

Camping: It is possible to camp near the Fuente del Home Mort, and there is a terraced camping area behind the Núria complex to the NNW, with toilets and showers on the west side of the bar below. The camping ground has been prepared with fine gravel and takes pegs with difficulty, so some protection for groundsheets is required, and rocks help with pitching. There is plenty of grass about but for decoration only.

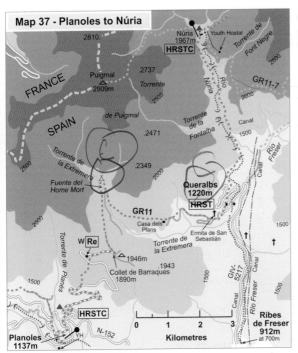

Map 37 - Planoles to Núria

up to the main road reaches the east one, with the GR11 route just out of sight to the left. From the bar/restaurant follow the tarmac road up to the main road. Ignore the concrete road ahead. Turn left and in a few metres turn right, N, up the cement road. Or, from the main square take one of the streets left, N, to locate the GR. A few minutes along the cement road take the right branch, NE, and in a few more minutes it climbs steeply to join a tarmac road above. *This comes from the other cement road via a long detour.* Turn left, NW, and follow this narrow road as it serpentines upward, passing Camping Can Fosset. About 3km later, while travelling NW, it makes a hairpin turn back SE, with a *pista* leaving to the N. *The small short-cut across this bend is no longer in*

Núria gorge

Waterfall, Núria gorge

use. Follow the bend around and in a few minutes take the waymarked route off to the left, NNE, which climbs steeply up through the forest. *The road continues to the same spot above, but is very much longer (though much easier) and passes a water point.* The trail arrives at the road, crosses it and continues to climb NNE, soon reaching a water point and picnic area with hut to the left. **1.45 Refugio, 1810m.** *The refugio has become dirty, as the doors have been left open and livestock have entered. Also, the water has all but stopped flowing. From above the hut the GR11, for some unaccountable reason, used to climb NE to a ridge and come down to the collado but now no longer does so.* From the hut go up to the road and follow it E to…

2.00 Collet de les Barraques, 1890m. *End of road and junction of* pistas. Go down the *pista* to the NW, which turns to the N and in 10mins comes to a grassy place. The trail has now been clearly marked, going straight on, slightly W of N. It passes through trees to easily descend to the…

2.40 Crossing of the Torrente de la Extremera, 1800m. *Camping possible here, near to Fuente del Home Mort.*

Cross the river, go along a trail SSE to the *pista*, in about 6mins, and almost immediately take the waymarked path going down to the right, SSE. At various junctions the route usually goes right. Twenty minutes later, after a stream, at a grassy place, go SE to pick up the path again passing a small hut over on the left. In another 20mins a farm on the right is passed. Go down E, with the farm *pista* to the right, to join it and pass around a bend to take a short-cut off left, NNE. This joins with the *pista* again shortly, crosses a bridge over the stream and continues SE then E for about 1km. Then keep an eye out for a new route, a waymarked path that leads to...

4.00 Queralbs, 1220m. *Hotels, bars, restaurants, telephone and shops for provisions.* **Note:** *The shop tends to close for the afternoon well before 2pm. These services are found in the lower part of town to the south, below which lies the station of the rack railway to Núria or down to Ribes de Freser and the main line.* Return to the upper road by cobbled streets and turn right for a short way before taking the *pista* N, signposted 'Cami de Núria'. Shortly, at a branch, take the *pista* ascending left, NNE, which looks as though it is only the access to the house seen above. Leave the house to the right and the *pista* becomes stony then later turns into a path, which reaches a road. Turn right for a few metres before turning off left and continuing the climb up the path, N. The railway comes into view below on the right, and the trail continues beside it for a while before crossing to the other side as the railway track passes into a tunnel.

Rack railway to Núria

Núria

The path then goes down to the Río Núria to cross it by the Pont del Cremat to continue the ascent of the left side of the valley, gaining height by zigzags in the gorge. After the gradient has eased the trail passes beneath the track by a small tunnel to continue climbing along the right side. Much later the path leads to the top of the last hill, called Creu d'en Riba. *Somehow the railway track has managed to avoid climbing this last obstacle. I expect that you also will be stunned at what you see – a huge man-made ski and holiday complex, surrounded by such striking beauty, in the middle of nowhere.* Go down to cross the Torrente de Finestrelles to arrive at…

6.30 Santuario de Núria, 1967m. *Hotel with restaurant, two bars, shop and rack-railway station adjacent. Camping area to NW with nearby cafe, toilets and showers. Youth hostel above by cable car. Cheap meals can be obtained in the main bar.*

DAY 38
Núria – Setcases

Maps: Editorial Alpina Puigmal. ICC Nos 31 & 2, Ripolles and Alt Empordá. Prames maps (1:40,000 and 1:50,000) 39.

Camping: No official camping areas after Núria, though places can be found up to 2400m.

Distance:	21km (13.1 miles)
Height gain:	1080m
Height loss:	1780m
Time:	6hrs 20mins

Today is unique in that, although well to the east of the highest mountains, the GR11 attains its greatest height as it passes along the border ridge for over 3km, with extensive views in clear weather. This ridge could be difficult to navigate in cloud and even more so in cloud with snow covering. But there are no such problems in good weather.

0.00 Santuario de Núria, 1967m. From behind the complex go NE to cross a small stone bridge and then

Profile Day 38

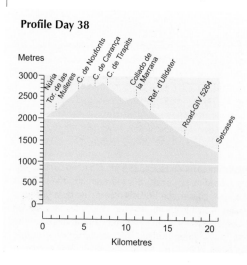

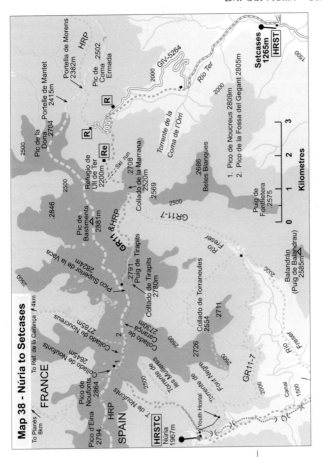

Map 38 - Núria to Setcases

follow the marks across grass and up a steep bank to join
the ascending *pista*, which is followed NE. *The valley to
the north goes to the Collado d'Eina.* The *pista* becomes
a path, which leads into the Torrente de las Mulleres de
Noucreus valley. At the entrance, a little below to the
left, is a wooden bridge. *This was broken but usable
during my visits.* Cross the bridge and go a few metres up

Looking towards Collado de la Marrana

NW to locate the trail climbing to the right by a series of large zigzags. The route is clearly marked as it climbs to the left side of the Torrente de Noufonts valley, at first in a northerly direction and then NE. A clear path climbs the final scree slope to...

1.45 Collado de Noufonts, 2645m. *Joined by the HRP from the left.* Turn right and climb the ridge SE, passing a small stone shelter seen to the left *(igloo type, useful as shelter in bad weather)*. Over the summit ridge of Pico de Noucreus, 2809m, the route turns to the E down to the Collado de Noucreus. It then turns ESE, then NE, to gain Pico de la Fossa del Gegant, 2805m. Go down ESE to the Collado de Carença, 2730m, and up again ESE to the Pic Superior de la Vaca, 2824m, though this can be avoided to the right before reaching the summit. *(This summit is the highest point on the GR11.)* From here leave the ridge turning to the right, E, and with little descent reach...

3.00 Collado de Tirapits, 2780m. *If the descent looks too intimidating in snow, an easy descent over grass can be found to the north, NNE from Pic Superior de la*

Vaca. Go down steeply N and then continue E across the hanging valley, passing a small stream at about 2400m before climbing the pass to the E, between Puig de Bastiments to the NW and Pic Gra de Fajol to the SE, called…

3.55 Collado de la Marrana, 2520m. *Care is needed, early in the season. Beware of cornices! In snow, the trail contours from the right of the pass to descend the right side of the valley below.* Once in the valley, the route goes down easily and across a wide ski piste to…

4.25 Refugio de Ull de Ter, 2200m. *Guardian during the summer with bar and meals. Bothy for 8 open when refugio is closed.* Continue E from the hut, crossing the stream below by a small plank bridge. The path arrives at the road; avoiding a steep gully on the right, go down easily, with the road zigzags on the left. At the last bend of the road, above a large parking area, follow the road down to cross the river and immediately take the trail on the right (waymarks eventually appear). If using the bar/restaurant seen below the bridge, there is a track beside the power pylon that goes down to the GR11. Follow the track down the left side of the river for about 3km, where it passes a hut over on the left, in good condition, before the now wide track meets the road again at a hairpin bend. Follow the road, ESE at first, which follows the River Ter, crossing to the right side just before arriving at…

6.20 Setcases, 1265m. *Hotels, bar/restaurants, shop and telephone.*

No Camp
Stay at Ull de Ter

DAY 39
Setcases – Beget

Maps: Editorial
Alpina Costabona.
ICC Nos 31 & 2,
Ripolles and Alt
Empordá. Prames
maps (1:40,000 and
1:50,000) 40.

Camping: Camping
no longer allowed in
the meadows below
Beget, but it might
be possible to camp
below the Torrente
de Bellistil, 2km into
the next stage.

Distance:	22km (13.7 miles)
Height gain:	820m
Height loss:	1575m
Time:	6hrs 30mins

The higher mountains behind, the route enters a more
verdant region today, and the highlight must be the long
descent from the Collado de Lliens across grassy ridges
down to Molló. Unless one has excellent navigation
skills it would be well not to cross the ridges in mist or
cloud. Water needs to be carried for the high section
until supplies can be replenished at Molló.

0.00 Setcases, 1265m. From the E of town cross the
bridge over the River Ter, taking the concrete road to a
steep, rough *pista* on the right, climbing E. Slightly to the

Profile Day 39

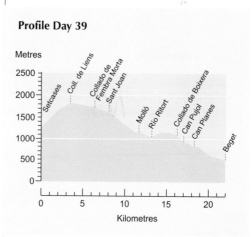

The church of St Cristofor, Beget

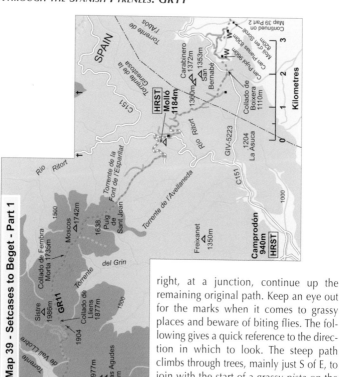

Map 39 - Setcases to Beget - Part 1

Río Ritort

SPAIN

Torrente de l'Abós

Torrente de la Ginebrosa

HRST
Molló
1184m

C-151

Carabinero
1372m

San
Bernabé
1360m △ 1353m

Collado de
Boixera
1110m

Río Ritort

GIV-5223

1204
La Asuca

Can Puig 960m

Molí d'en Soluli
820m

Continued on
Map 39 Part 2

W W

C151

Kilometres
0   1   2   3

1000

Camprodón
940m
HRST

Río Ritort

Torrente de la
Font de l'Espariat

Torrente de l'Avellaneda

Moscos
△1742m

1638
Puig
de
Sant Joan

1600

Freixanet
1350m

Collado de Fembra
Morta 1735m

Sistre
1986m

GR11

Collado de
Lliens
1877m

del Grin

Torrente

1904

Bach 1977m

Puig de las Agudes
1967m

Torrente de Vall Llobre

1500

1500

Setcases
1265m
HRST

right, at a junction, continue up the remaining original path. Keep an eye out for the marks when it comes to grassy places and beware of biting flies. The following gives a quick reference to the direction in which to look. The steep path climbs through trees, mainly just S of E, to join with the start of a grassy *pista* on the other side of a stream. At the first grassy place it crosses E then continues ESE. Later, at a meadow, it goes steeply up, SE, to locate a path going E, then goes S up a grassy path to another going E again. Then proceed ESE up steep grass to a path turning northwards. At the next grass go E, turning SE to climb beside a stream which is crossed beside a wire-cage, stone-retaining wall across the stream. Go along the *pista*, NE then ENE, for 8–9mins where, at waymarks, you turn up the mountainside using the left side (true right side) of a rocky gully. The pass lies SE from here. Continue steeply upwards to the top of the gully. Here, look out for waymarks leading left, E, to a depression between two small hills at…

1.40 Collado de Lliens, 1877m. Cross the fence and contour ENE across the south slopes of Sistre. There are a number of tracks to choose from, with waymarks from time to time. The trail looses a little height, and the correct line used to be identified by a large quartz boulder ahead, which is still there but hidden by new trees. This is still some way before reaching the SE ridge from Sistre. Once on the ridge, or just to the right of it, go down SE, with a fence on the left, and in about 10mins reach…

2.05 Collado de la Fembra Morta, 1735m. *The path continues SE below a high point on the ridge called Moscos, 1742m. It would be very easy to become lost below Moscos in mist. The main ridge divides into two parts going S. The first and westerly part carries the path that the GR11 has been using, only now descending S. The second soon also divides, with one branch going SE. The GR crosses E from one ridge to the other and then takes the SE branch.* As the ridge begins to turn S keep an eye out to the left for marks on posts of the wire fence which indicate the way through. Continue ESE 500m to a second fence on the other ridge. On the other side turn S with the fence on the right. Some 200m later, with the shallow lump of Puig de Sant Joan on the right, the faint track turns to the left, SE, to find a *pista* which is followed down the ridge. Follow all the way down SE and finally S, at a junction, for a short way to the road. Turn left down the road which turns N before crossing the stream and climbs steeply SE through…

3.20 Molló, 1184m. *Hotels, bar/restaurants, shops, telephone.* From the top of town turn left down the road NNE which goes to the main road. Turn right, S, along this road to the Hostal Françoise. Turn left immediately beyond the *hostal*, going down a *pista* SSE. Go straight on through an iron gate with a 'Private' notice and follow GR11 and GR65 variant waymarks to a concrete road. Turn left to the bridge over the…

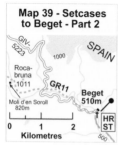

Map 39 - Setcases to Beget - Part 2

3.40 Río Ritort, 1050m. Climb the *pista* SE on the other side, ignoring turnings to the left or right. It climbs to fields, and when approaching power lines keep left, SE, after crossing a stream. Ascend slightly to reach a T-junction. *To the right, the farm Can Querol can be seen.* Leave the *pistas* and go straight on, SE, across the fields, spotting waymarks on trees, to a small stream below. Cross the stream and continue along a path SE. A few minutes later the path joins a *pista* to the road at...

4.30 Collado de la Boixera, 1110m. Cross the road and locate the waymarked path going down E into the wood, not the obvious *pista* going SE. Soon cross a stream and then turn down left, E. Do not follow the path into the field ahead. At a fallen tree turn left, NE, to soon join the *pista* going N passing Can Pujol, seen on the right. The *pista* soon turns E, avoiding a *pista* to the left, then turns S then E. Look out for a new signposted way across fields to the right. Follow this track to a field and turn right to locate the path a short distance away, which

Beget

joins the *pista* again. Turn sharp right, S, and in a few minutes arrive at…

5.05 Can Planas, 830m. Just before the main building take a *pista* for a short way and then a path left, SE. Follow the marks past various buildings to drop steeply down to the Camprodon–Beget road. *The Spanish Guide says turn right and follow the road to Beget while showing the road in a different position on the map. The 1:40,000 map now shows the road in the correct place, but the GR11 is still ambiguous.* Cross the road and go down to the stream, crossing by a quaint and ancient stone bridge, and continue along the left bank of the Río Llierca. A little later cross to the right-hand bank by another stone bridge and climb back up to the road once more. Turn either left and follow the road to the village, or turn right a short distance and follow marks climbing into the wood on the opposite side of the road. This returns to the road later for about 100m before turning left down a track which avoids the last bends of the road, returning to the road for the last few metres into…

6.30 Beget, 510m. *A pretty village, almost deserted outside of the holiday season. The 12th-century church, dedicated to Sant Cristofor, is a national monument. There is a hostal, bar/restaurants and a small shop in season. Out of season Can Joanic should be open, except Tuesdays (tel: 972 741 241/mobile 989-500 302), or find the bar to the NE of the village.*

DAY 40
Beget – Sant Aniol d'Aguja

Maps: Editorial Alpina Garrotxa. ICC Nos 31 & 2, Ripolles and Alt Empordá. Prames maps (1:40,000 and 1:50,000) 41. Please note that some maps show Sant Aniol d'Aguja on the wrong side of the river.

Camping: Below Torrente de Bellistil and at Sant Aniol.

Distance:	16.5km (10.3 miles)
Height gain:	690m
Height loss:	740m
Time:	4hrs 40mins

A varied route of paths and *pistas* arrive at the remains of the Benedictine monastery established in the ninth century. Just below Les Feixanes, I met two young Australians who had been walking 10 days, only seeing one pair of backpackers in that time. I had been walking eight days, and they were the first I had seen! Provisions for two days are needed. From now on, it is important to carry sufficient water, as springs are frequently dry during the summer.

0.00 Beget, 510m. From the square beside the church go S down the waymarked *pista* on the right of the stream. Shortly cross the river by a stone bridge and continue SE, ignoring a *pista* going up left and another going right over a bridge. There are several concrete sections along this *pista*. Camping possible below the junction with the Torrente de Bellistil. Avoid another *pista* off left here. Ignore yet another, left, later but follow the *pista* that fords the River Llierca to reach...

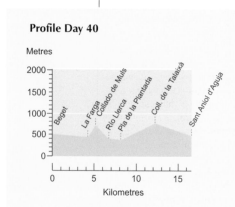

Profile Day 40

Metres

Beget — La Farga — Collado de Muls — Río Llierca — Pla de la Plantada — Coll. de la Talaixà — Sant Aniol d'Aguja

0   5   10   15

Kilometres

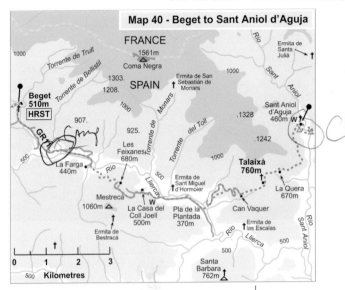

Map 40 - Beget to Sant Aniol d'Aguja

0.45 La Farga, 440m. *Large inhabited building*. Below the buildings, take the marked path across the Rabassa stream and follow the path up through the trees, SSE then SE, to a pass called Coll dels Muls, 700m. Follow the path to pass through the ruined buildings ahead called...

1.30 Les Feixanes, 680m. Follow the *pista* down SW on the other side of the ruins. This turns SE and, going down, bends to the NE, then passes the track to the left going to Coll Joell and, a few minutes later, a spring on the right in the wood. Some minutes later ignore a *pista* to the left but continue following the right-hand bank of the Río Llierca. Ten minutes later bear right at a junction, SE, and then as the valley narrows ahead keep an eye open for the waymarked path left at a meadow, with signpost on the left...

2.25 Pla de la Plantada, 370m. Turn left, E, cross the river and pick up the trail climbing NE through the wood. Shortly it joins a *pista* at a bend. Go up NE and in a moment the trail takes to a path to the right climbing

On the way to Sant Aniol d'Aguja

steeply ENE through undergrowth. If the track is over-grown, continue on the *pista*, which also climbs steeply in places as it makes a bend to the N to join with the GR later. The path joins the *pista* again. Turn right and climb the *pista* NE and around bends to Can Vaquer. Continue by a path ENE on the left of the house and follow the marks to…

3.35 Collado de Talaixà, 760m. *A church and ruined village above on the left contains a water point. Probably dry during the summer.* Go down N then NE to the ruin of La Quera. Exit up left and the trail continues ENE and, having turned NNW, climbs above the crags called Salt de la Núvia. Descend then, turning NE, pass through a gate and follow the trail turning E to…

4.40 Sant Aniol d'Aguja, 460m. *Church unlocked and with interesting cave below. The water point only flows slowly. If dry, water must be obtained from the river below, behind the church. There is an open-fronted arch suitable for bivouac and camping in the old terraced meadows. This is a very busy place during the summer, at weekends, due to canyonning in the local rivers. Having replenished water supplies, there is a quieter field a short distance into the next day at the southern tip of El Brull.*

DAY 41
Sant Aniol d'Aguja – Albanyà

Distance:	18km (11.2 miles)
Height gain:	685m
Height loss:	910m
Time:	6hrs 15mins

Maps: Editorial Alpina Garrotxa. ICC No 2, Alt Empordà. Prames maps (1:40,000 and 1:50,000) 42.

Pleasant forest trails, though not so pleasant during or after rain, lead finally to the *pista* at Can Nou and easy ground for the long way down to Albanyà. Water will be needed to last all day, as replenishment cannot be guaranteed at either Can Galan or Can Nou.

Camping: Camping Bassegoda west of Albanyà, open all year, except at Christmas. Restaurant and bar service.

0.00 Sant Aniol d'Aguja, 460m. Follow the path down SE for about 3mins and cross the Río Sant Aniol below and on the left. Follow the path on the other side as it climbs round to the NW along the right bank of the Comella valley, avoiding the path going S. The clearly marked path climbs well above the river, which is a bit disconcerting, as one expects it to be crossing the water.

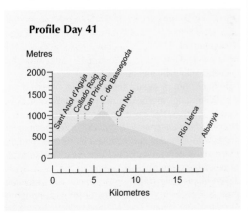

213

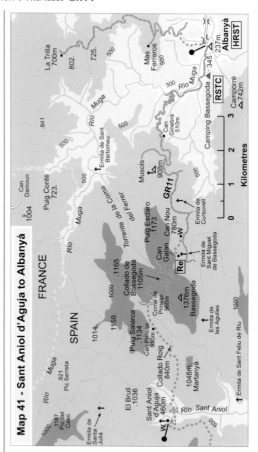

Map 41 - Sant Aniol d'Aguja to Albanyà

However, persevere; and soon, from the left bank of the Torrente de la Comella, the route climbs E through the trees, signpost to Albanyà. Higher, it crosses a scree slope before reaching...

1.30 Collado Roig, 840m. Turn left, NE, and follow the path as it contours the slope, then climbs, passing Can Principi about 30mins later. Continue NW to the head of the valley, where the stream bed is crossed. The trail leads steeply upward ESE for about 3mins to join a grassy *pista,* SE, which soon leads to a ruin on the right. Take the marked, ascending path to the left, ENE, being careful to spot two sharp left turns, which access higher paths. The first is obscured by small pines and is only a short way from the ruin. Waymarks confirm the correct paths that climb to the *pista* above. Turn right, SE, a little later, avoiding the turning going right to Bassegoda, 1379m, to reach…

2.55 Collado de Bassegoda, 1105m. Continue across the pass for a few minutes before it descends SE, ignoring two *pista*s to the left. About 100m from the second *pista* turn left, E, down a well-marked path through the wood (GR11 signpost to Sant Aniol). The path zigzags steeply down passing Can Galan (Refugio de Bassegoda) over on the right. *A mountain hut with dubious bottled water and about 20 places.* Continue down to the buildings of…

4.00 Can Nou, 780m. Follow the *pista* E, passing a water point on the left after 300m, the Fuente de Can Nou, dry in the summer, and a *pista* to the right a few minutes later. Much later, as the GR *pista* turns north once more, ignore the *pista* to the right and then, about 10mins later, below Musols, 908m, turn sharp right, SW, at a junction. Follow the *pista* down as it makes a large loop back to the E again. More zigzags lead down to the Río Muga, where at the T-junction you turn right, S, following the *pista* along the right bank of the river. This leads past the large and well-appointed campsite, Camping Bassegoda, and on to cross the bridge just a few minutes from…

6.15 Albanyà, 237m. *Small village with hotel, restaurant and several bars and telephone.*

DAY 42
Albanyà – La Vajol

Maps: SGE 38-11 and 38-10. ICC No 2, Alt Empordà. Exit from Albanyà incorrect on Prames and ICC maps. Prames maps (1:40,000 and 1:50,000) 43.

Camping: Possibility at Molí d'en Robert and at La Vajol, at the car park at the lower end of the village. There are two fields above and to the SE.

Distance:	27km (16.8 miles)
Height gain:	860m
Height loss:	550m
Time:	6hrs 20mins

From Albanyà the GR goes northwards to maintain high ground through a nice mix of forest paths and *pistas*. Hopefully, with the navigation problems solved, it will be a very pleasant, though long, walk. Water supplies can be replenished just below Mas Rimalo. Please note that there have been four main changes to the original route. Continental guides show the route from Albanyà ascending from the wrong road bridge. They also make a loop to pass by Mas Ferreros, but it is not necessary to do this. Also, the route has been substantially changed from Molí d'en Robert, no doubt due to the rescinding of the right of way by Can Vall. On the outskirts of Massanet de Cabrenys the route to the road has moved further to the

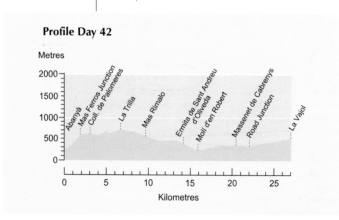

Profile Day 42

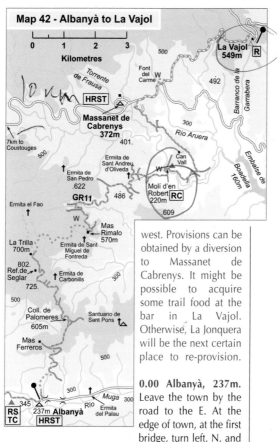

Map 42 - Albanyà to La Vajol

0   1   2   3
Kilometres

Torrente de Frausa

Font del Carme **W**

500

La Vajol 549m R

492

Barranco de la Garrabera

HRST

Massanet de Cabrenys 372m

7km to Coustouges

500

401.

300

Rio Aruera

Embalse de Boadella 160m

Ermita de Sant Andreu d'Oliveda †

Ermita de San Pedro .622

GR11

486

W

Can Vall

W

Moli d'en Robert 220m RC

609

Ermita el Fao †

Mas Rimalo 570m

La Trilla 700m

Ermita de Sant Miguel de Fontreda †

802. Ref.de Seglar

Ermita de Carbonills †

725.

500

300

Coll. de Palomeres 605m

Santuario de Sant Pons

Mas Ferreros

500

▲ 345

300

Muga

300

RS TC

237m **Albanyà**

Rio

Ermita del Palau †

HRST

west. Provisions can be obtained by a diversion to Massanet de Cabrenys. It might be possible to acquire some trail food at the bar in La Vajol. Otherwise, La Jonquera will be the next certain place to re-provision.

0.00 Albanyà, 237m. Leave the town by the road to the E. At the edge of town, at the first bridge, turn left, N, and follow the well-marked *pista*, at first, then footpath, which follows the right bank of the stream for a short distance before climbing steeply to the left. After about 30mins it comes upon a *pista* which is followed upwards, N, for about 2mins before taking a short-cut straight on N across a bend of this *pista*. Cross the *pista* and continue to climb the path N, which soon joins the *pista* yet again, which is followed left, NW, and on to a sharp right bend. Just after this bend turn left, N, to climb a path through the wood. This comes upon the *pista* again where one turns left, NW, for a short distance before reaching a junction at open ground. Slightly left, the *pista* goes to Mas Ferreros but the GR11 turns right, NE, along an earth *pista*. In about 10mins, at a junction, this *pista* arrives at…

1.15 Collado de Palomeres, 605m. Take the left branch, NNW, and follow it as it contours, more or less, the slopes ahead, passing La Ermita de Carbonils, seen down to the right. About 10mins later the Refugio de Seglar is seen to the left. Private hut, locked and no water outside, but with tables under shelter. Continue NNW to…

2.05 La Trilla, 700m. Leave the *pista* for a path entering the woods NE. Don't take the one going NNW. Follow the waymarks as the trail turns N, then E, and N and E again to cross a small stream and drop down to the ruins of Mas Rimalo. At the *pista*, turn left, N, signposted to Albanyà, avoiding a turning on the right. About 4mins later pass a water point on the left and continue along the *pista*, avoiding turns to the left and then turns to the right, as indicated on the sketch map. This eventually reaches the complex of…

3.40 Ermita de Sant Andreu d'Oliveda, 380m. Take the *pista* E and follow down to and across the stream to…

4.00 Molí d'en Robert, 220m. *Picnic area, swimming pool, bar/restaurant and small campsite in season. Nothing open, except during the summer.* **Note: the route no longer leaves to the N.** Just above the buildings, turn right, SE, and follow the *pista* for some time before other waymarks appear. Avoid a turning left after 700m, but turn left, N, at the next junction. The *pista* then ascends to join another a few minutes later. Turn sharp left, NW, and follow the *pista* N and NW to higher open farmland where, after 1km, the old route joins from the left. Continue NW to the edge of Massanet de Cabrenys. Avoid the concrete road going down steeply to the right, which was the old way, but continue on, following the marks past the football pitch over on the right. Turn right, N, at the first housing access road. Shortly leave the road to the right and then left to follow a path beside fields, which joins a farm *pista* for about 150m before joining the main road. *To the left, ESE, is Massanet de Cabrenys with all the usual services.* Turn right and follow the road for 1km to the Barranco de Can Rey, where the road turns sharply to the south. Cross the bridge and turn left, N, following a path to…

5.15 Font del Carme, 330m. *Water point.* Turn right, E, and go up the track to join a *pista*, which almost immediately joins the road coming up from just beyond the bridge. Follow this road E, as it climbs generally to the NE all the way to…

6.20 La Vajol, 549m. *The road arrives at a large restaurant above to the left. The village lies below to the right. There are two other restaurant/bars in the old village, but no accommodation. There is a* hostal, *but it is closed. Camping in the fields is possible. Water can be had from a fountain beside the Jewish memorial, at the bottom of the steps, at the southern end of the village. Enquiry might gain access to some shelter, set aside for GR11 walkers.*

DAY 43
La Vajol – Requesens

Maps: SGE 39-10.
ICC No 2, Alt
Empordà. Prames
maps (1:40,000 and
1:50,000) 44.

Camping: Campsites
at La Jonquera and in
meadows below
Requesens

Distance:	24.5km (15.2 miles)
Height gain:	830m
Height loss:	880m
Time:	6hrs 20mins

The day of the *pista*! Mostly on *pistas*, the route comes down to the large road marshalling area to the north of La Jonquera to pass under the motorway into the town. Then it passes over the ridge to the east to reach Requesens. The climb over the ridge may be easy or difficult, depending on the encroachment of thorn bushes.

0.00 La Vajol, 549m. Take the road from the car park going down NW, which later turns E, and follow it for 3.3km where waymarks indicate a turn left, N, along a *pista*. This soon joins another coming from the right. Turn left, NW, and go along this *pista*, which turns NE passing Mas Carreres, avoiding the turns to the left and right indicated on the sketch map, to arrive at...

Profile Day 43

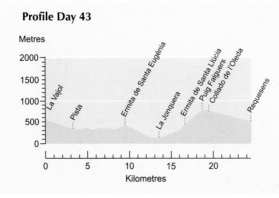

220

1.30 Ermita de Santa Eugénia, 350m. Take the *pista* ESE, which in about 10mins arrives at a junction. Turn left, NNW. A few minutes later the water point of Can Marine is passed (probably dry during the summer). The *pista* crosses a stream and begins to climb. At a junction, at the top of the hill, turn right, SE. The route continues E, and in about 10mins turn right, SE, at another junction.

The *pista* continues generally SE, and in a further 15–20mins turn right at a *pista* joining from the left. In another 10–15mins, turn SE at a junction.

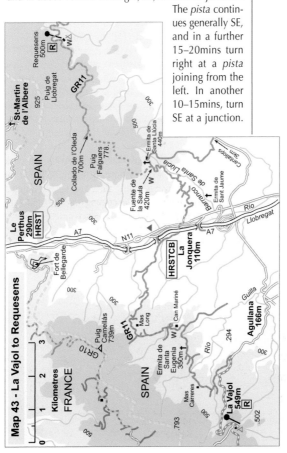

Map 43 - La Vajol to Requesens

Ten minutes or so later, the waymarks indicate a turn left to cross a bridge over the motorway, but it is better to turn right, SE, alongside a wire fence, unless the Hypermarket is required on the main road. This route is waymarked also. About 15mins later this turns left to an underpass and to a bridge over the Río Llobregat and the centre of…

3.15 La Jonquera, 110m. *A town adjacent to the customs check area on the motorway. All normal facilities can be found. The best supermarkets are beyond the bridge turning right, S. Sufficient provisions will be needed in order to reach Llançà, which is the next re-provisioning point. Meals can probably be had at Requesens and at Sant Quirze de Colera.* Cross the bridge and turn right, S, and after some 250m turn left and climb steeply to the SE of town by way of Carrer Cantallops, La Plaça del Sol and Carrer Jossello, which leads to a *pista*, soon taking the left branch. New, useable short-cuts have been waymarked between various sections of the *pista*. Please refer to the

View from Ermita de Sant Llúcia

sketch map. Climbing the right-hand side of the Barranco de Sant Llúcia, the *pista* twists and turns, generally NE. When in sight of Ermita de Sant Llúcia, take the path to the left, NNE, and then left again, NNW, steeply to...

4.15 Fuente de la Saula, 420m. *An essential water point in hot weather! Fine views to the coast and the Gulf of Rosas from beside the hermitage. This has become a popular barbecue site in summer. The* pista *coming from the Cantallops road has been surfaced on the steepest places.* Go up the steps opposite the water point, turning left to find waymarks leading to a clear path going NW, climbing through thorn bushes. The trail climbs generally NE now and passes just below the summit of...

5.10 Puig Falguers, 778m. Continue N passing some rocky outcrops on their western side, turning NE to go down to the *pista* below, near to the Collado de l'Oleda, 700m. Turn right and follow the main *pista* down. *There is a memorial to the French aircrew lost in a DC 6 crash in 1986, just as the track steepens, with the aircraft remains still perched high above.* Follow the *pista* to the small hamlet of...

6.20 Requesens, 500m. *Popular traditional bar/ restaurant. Water point on the left before reaching the buildings and another below, SW, among terraces just suitable for camping. The resident bull seems quite harmless! It might be possible to use the toilet and shower behind the bar/restaurant.*

DAY 44
Requesens – St Quirze de Colera

Maps: SGE 39-10 and 40-10. ICC No 2, Alt Empordà. Prames maps (1:40,000 and 1:50,000) 45.

Distance:	26km (16.2 miles)
Height gain:	575m
Height loss:	910m
Time:	6hrs 15mins

Camping: At Sant Quirze de Colera

A long but gentle day with no major climbs, passing mostly through open countryside. Care with navigation will be required only off *pista*. A lot of ground is covered due to the extent of *pistas* used. Excitement mounts as the coast is seen ever closer! **Note: The heat now can become a problem in summer. The only water points that can be expected to be still flowing will be those above and below below Els Vilars.**

0.00 Requesens, 500m. From the bar, take the *pista* going down N passing the Fuente el Ferro and picnic area a few minutes later. The *pista* turns SE, and in few

Profile Day 44

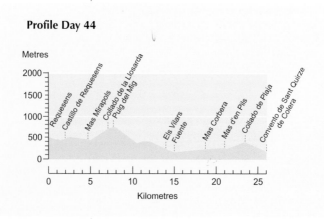

224

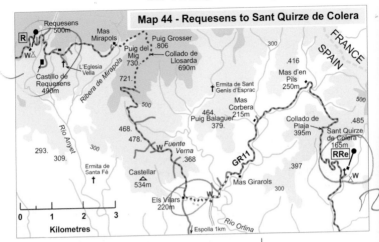

Map 44 - Requesens to Sant Quirze de Colera

minutes pass another on the left closed by an iron gate. A few metres later turn left from the main *pista* to another *pista* going N. This soon crosses a wooden bridge and turns to the SE. Take the right fork here, which crosses another stream and climbs to the junction to Castillo de Requesens on the right. *The castle now is open to the public for a small fee, but does not open until 10.00am. A key is available at the bar, but a car is needed in order to return it there.* Go straight on E, with the stone wall on the right. In about 10mins turn left, N, at another junction. Follow this *pista* all the way to Mas Mirapols. A path leads down NNE to Ribera de Mirapols. On the other side, the path first turns S, then ENE and again turning S to reach…

1.50 Collado de Llosarda, 690m. *Fine views in good weather and from various points along the top of the ridge.* The marked way continues SW on the western side of the ridge until below Puig del Mig, 730m, marks lead through a fence on the left. Take care here to find the correct route. *Once the trail went E from here but does so no longer.* Immediately after crossing the fence turn right, S, to find a clear marked path, but very soon take a

225

The castle of Requesens with the Mediterranean in the distance

less distinct branch to the left, S, and the waymarks lead to the left, E, of the rocky high ground ahead, the Puig de Roureda, 721m. Follow the path down, S, to join a *pista* and turn right, W. Follow this *pista* down as it turns generally SSE, ignoring various turnings. Cross a stream and ascend a little, and as the *pista* turns to the E, Fuente Verna with tap and picnic table is on the left. Then follow the *pista* all the way to…

3.30 Els Vilars, 220m. Leave the *pista* for a track on the left, E, which goes down to a stream. Take care to spot the waymarks here. Cross the stream and follow a clear path SE, which soon turns left along a not-so-clear path beside the stream. About 20mins from Els Vilars, this path comes to a road at the Fuente de Cadecas. *The water quality is not too good in summer.* Go straight up the narrow road, which soon becomes a *pista* with one or two concrete sections. *A road is under construction in 2003, which may go as far as Mas Corbera.* After about 10–12mins, waymarks indicate a path to the right, E, used as a short-cut. Soon join the *pista* again going NE. Mas Girarols is seen off to the right. Then much later…

Mas Corbera

4.30 Mas Corbera, 215m. Seen on the left. Take the right branch of the *pista* which crosses the Torrente de Freixa and continues NE to Mas d'en Pils on the left. Follow the *pista* to the right, S, or cut across the arid fields to cross the Rio Orlina and go up the other side, generally SSE, and with a turn to the right, SW, reach the obvious pass ahead...

5.40 Collado de Plaja, 395m. Follow the *pista* S to the old monastery seen among the fields below. Lower down, the trail makes a number of zigzags before arriving at...

6.15 Monasterio de Sant Quirze de Colera, 165m. *There is a bar/restaurant here, run by Luis and Christina. It may be possible to use the shower in the ladies toilet. The bothy within the monastery may also still be in use. If camping, there is a spring higher up to the E among the terraces. There may still be a tap near to the monastery.*

227

DAY 45
St Quirze de
Colera – El Port de la Selva

Maps: SGE 40-10 and 40-11. ICC No 2, Alt Empordà. Prames maps (1:40,000 and 1:50,000) 45 and 46.

Camping: Campsites at Llançà and near to El Port de la Selva

Distance:	27km (16.8 miles)
Height gain:	775m
Height loss:	925m
Time:	6hrs 40mins

There is a sting in the tail of the GR11. As it arrives near to the coast it turns south to climb nearly 500m to the monastery of Sant Pere de Roda. This is set on the upper north-facing slopes of Roda, 670m, and overlooking El Port de la Selva. The monastery is undergoing some form of restoration. There are plenty of places at Llançà in which one can refuel for the climb. This will be a long but pleasant day with views over the coast. It is also possible to follow the GR92 waymarked coastal route to El Port de la Selva, instructions below.

0.00 Monestario de Sant Quirze de Colera, 165m. Take the obvious *pista* southward all the way to…

Profile Day 45

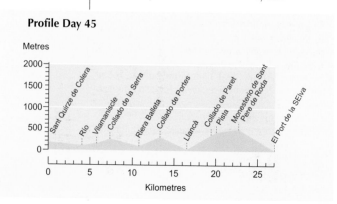

228

1.15 Vilamaniscle, 155m (169m at top of village). *Good water point at the entrance to the village. No other facilities here.* Take the second turning left, NE, which climbs steeply to the edge of town. Near the top, take a left then right to follow the signs to 'Las Casas de Colonies Tramuntana'. This large holiday centre is soon passed and the marks appear. Continue NE climbing to the...

1.40 Collado de la Serra, 260m. Take the *pista* left, N, which goes down, soon turning SE, avoiding a *pista* to the left. About 2km later, cross the Riera Balleta. Avoid the level *pista* to the left which goes to the Ermita de Sant Silvestre, but climb the other one going NW then NE above Sant Silvestre, with its vast area of ancient terraces that are now overgrown. Continue the climb to the...

2.45 Collado de les Portes, 230m. *Llançà and the sea seen to the east.* Take the left *pista*, E then generally ESE, all the way down to the main road. *The route no longer goes along the main road to the town but works its way through the small streets to the west.* Cross the road to waymarks

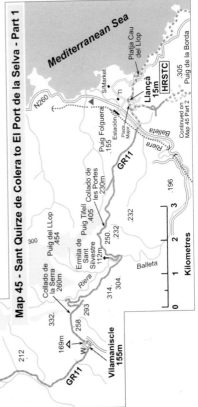

229

Beach at Llanca

and follow Carrer Compte Jofre and C. Nicolas Salmerón to the centre for provisions.

3.30 Llançà, 15m. *All necessary facilities. For the coastal route, follow C. Compte Jofre, on the eastern side of route N-260. This leads to C. Nicolas Salmerón and the Plaça Major. Exit along C. Rafael Estela and cross C. Gardissó, turning right along C. Cabrafiga. Turn left and climb C. El Colomer; to avoid using the main coastal road, at the roundabout turn right up C. Montserrat. Turn down left at C. Abat Escarré and cross the main road. Go down C. Empúries, taking the first on the right, C. Venturer, and the first waymarks to some steps that lead down to the beach of Platja Cau del Llop. Go part-way across the beach to the ascending road that soon leads to the path down along the coast, the GR 92.* From the centre, go back along C. Nicolas Salmerón to the west. Then go first left, S, C. Nord, keeping left at a fork into C. Aforca. Turn right at the end to see C. Sant Pere de Roda going S. Follow this to a *pista* and shortly go right at a fork, then straight across at a crossing. After a streambed the *pista* steepens, S, and waymarks lead along a track ahead. There are various path junctions as indicated on the sketch map. The path climbs steeply to reach an obvious pass called...

4.40 Collado de Paret, 360m. Turn right, SW, and climb the steep vegetated ridge. In about 10–15mins, depending on how hot and tired you feel, the path arrives at a welcome *pista*. Turn left, SE, and follow this to the El Port de la Selva to Vilajuiga road. Turn left, SE, and follow to the entrance of...

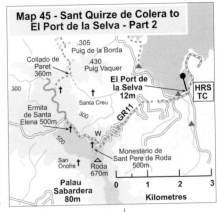

Map 45 - Sant Quirze de Colera to El Port de la Selva - Part 2

5.35 Monasterio de Sant Pere de Roda, 500m. Pass through the gate and walk down the new sloping apron on the north side of the monastery. *A short way down and below, on a small flat grassy platform, is a spring.*

Monasterio de Sant Pere de Roda

El Port de la Selva

Continue to the newly bulldozed *pista* and follow down to a large car parking area, which looks like a very wide road when empty. Continue down to the actual road and go straight across to find a path going straight down and across the many zigzags of the road. Sketch map shows details. The last section is somewhat thorny and awkward as it passes over old terrace-retaining stone walls, but does save a very long section of road. This arrives below at the roads and houses of Urbanizacion Euromar. Just follow the roads down to the main Llançà/El Port de la Selva road. *Turn left and continue for 1.7km to Camping Port de la Vall, open all year, though the restaurant will only be open during the holiday season. Turn right, then right again down the Cadaqués road for about 1km to Camping Port de la Selva, open June to September. There is a small site just to the right and opposite, but it, no doubt, will be full of water-sport campers in summer. Turn right, ESE, along the road to...*
6.40 El Port de la Selva, 12m. *Hotels, bar/restaurants, telephones and campsites nearby.*

DAY 46
El Port de la Selva – Cabo de Creus

Distance:	16km (9.9 miles)
Height gain:	445m
Height loss:	440m
Time:	4hrs 20mins

Maps: SGE 40-10 and 40-11. ICC No 2, Alt Empordà. Prames maps (1:40,000 and 1:50,000) 47. New route from Ermita de Sant Baldiri not marked on any maps. See sketch map!

Though near to the coast, this last day still retains the GR11 ambience of remoteness. There are mixed emotions now – sadness as this is the last of many days of wilderness wandering, and excitement in anticipation of returning to loved ones. Water will need to be carried for the whole day. The bar/restaurant, run by Chris Little, at Cabo Creus should be open during the summer. He does have a room for GR11 walkers (tel: 972 19 90 05). If this is not available or not wanted, then returning from Cabo de Creus to civilisation is a problem. Perhaps the best way is to stay two days at El Port, travel light and retrace one's steps. There is a bus from El Port to Llançà, or the pleasant coastal footpath, GR92, is an alternative. It is possible to walk or hitch to Cadaqués, from where buses go to Figueras. There is only one taxi here.

Profile Day 46

233

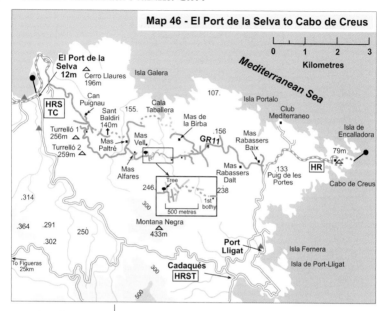

Map 46 - El Port de la Selva to Cabo de Creus

Camping: Due to the arid nature of the terrain it is not easy to camp. It may be possible to ask at one of the farms. Otherwise, there is a campsite at Port Lligat just NE of Cadaqués, if you are going that way, which is open during the summer only and has gravel pitches.

Hitching back to El Port is also possible from Cadaqués, though there is a long hill to climb, with most of the traffic going in the Figueras direction. **Please note that a new route has been waymarked from the southern side of Mas d'en Paltré to SE of Mas de la Birba. No way-marked routes connect with the old way from El Port de la Selva. Follow instructions below.**

0.00 El Port de la Selva, 12m. Follow the coast road N, the Carrer del Mar, and as it climbs the headland, marks appear. The road climbs steeply to the SE, while the road down left to the Cala Tamariua is ignored. Climb steeply up the road right, S, which soon becomes a *pista*. A little later pass a road coming up from the right. About 10mins later the *pista* makes a bend to the N before returning to the SE again. In another 10mins the access road to Can Puignau is passed on the left. Continue SE and in 5mins take the left fork, SE. In about 3mins turn left, E, along a wide path, and in a few minutes this comes upon a junction of *pistas*. Take the one going SE, which in a few minutes terminates at...

1.05 Ermita de Sant Baldiri, 140m. Continue along the path ESE, which curves around to the dry streambed of Riera Paltré where it turns left, N, to join with the *pista* coming from the right. *Note: The old route now terminates at Cala Tavallera and there is no waymarked exit route due to complaint from Mas de la Birba.* Turn right, SE, ignoring the No Way mark. Follow the *pista* past Mas d'en Paltré to a junction with signpost to Mas Vell and Mas Alfares and waymarks. Turn left, ESE, along *pista*, which in a few minutes passes Mas Alfares and turns down SE and then NNE. Follow the *pista* to a distinct tree on a rise. *Mas de la Birba can be seen across the valley.* Ignore a track left after the tree but follow the *pista* as it turns right, but leave this immediately for a path down left, NE. *Thorn bushes are not too much of a problem.* The path soon crosses an old *pista* and joins with another track, turning left. Then ignore a path and *pista* on the left. Some 40m after the *pista* take the right fork,

Cadaqués offers the nearest public transport to the end of the GR11

235

E. At the bottom, go S a couple of metres to locate the path, NE, to the next small valley. Climb out of this valley E then NE. Fork right, SSE, up the path, though both routes join later. As the slope eases, the path becomes a *pista* passing two stone bothies a few minutes apart. Ignoring a *pista* right, the trail joins another *pista*. Turn left and follow this round to the ENE. Ignore a *pista* on the left *(this has a No Way mark on a tree that is actually on the correct route, which is only confusing if walking from the east)* and continue to signpost. Go straight on, along the *pista* ENE to join the old route coming from Cala Tavellera. In a few minutes this reaches a solitary pine. Turn right, E, continuing along the *pista*. About 7mins later, at a junction, turn right, S, and follow the *pista* as it makes a turn to the N, passing an iron gate, before returning to the SE. Sometime later it passes the ruined Mas Rabassers Dalt, seen to the right, turning to the E to reach…

Approaching Cabo de Creus

3.10 Mas Rabassers Baix, 75m. The *pista* joins another crossing at right angles. Cross the grass straight ahead, E,

and follow the clear path now to climb up to the road, in a few minutes. Turn left, E, and ascend the road and follow it, undulating, past the left turn to the Club Mediterraneo and on to the neck of the final peninsula. Take the narrow steep cobbled path that climbs spectacularly across the south face of the cliff to reach the lighthouse area. Waymarks lead down E to a stone built bench overlooking the sea and Isla Masa de Oro at…

The stone seat and the end

4.20 Cabo de Creus, 15m. *The bar/restaurant is now open all year. See above for return suggestions. There is a bus from Cadaqués to Figueras that leaves just after 5pm. In Figueras there is an HI hostal on the west of town and a campsite 3km to the NNW, which is poor but with an excellent restaurant. All other services here too. There is also a bus from Cadaqués to El Port, but this is only of use if staying overnight in Cadaqués.*

Looking westward, Ordesa, GR11 seen below (Day 16)

GR11 VARIANTS

Short notes on alternative or access routes
The route descriptions in the guide do not always followed the official main route, as some variants have become the better way and are the most popular. Not all variants have acquired an individual route suffix, but where these are attributed, they have been noted.

Variant No.1. GR11.1 Selba d'Oza to Candanchù via Refugio de Lizara (Commencing Day 11). Two days are required with a stopover at the Refugio de Lizara. Go S to the Puen de Santa Ana, 920m. Then E to the Refugio de Lizara, 1540m. Continue E to Collado d'o Boxo, 2019m. Then SE to Collado de Riguelo, 2043m. SE to Canfranc and then N, using the GR65.3 variant, to join either the GR11 main route or the Collado de Izas variant.

Variant No.2. GR11 Candanchù to Sallent de Gállego via Cuello d'Izas (Day 12). Leave the main route at the Canal Roya entrance, going S then E into the Canal d'Izas and on to the Cuello d'Izas, 2230m. Go down NE and then ENE by *pista*, turning N along a path to join with the Canal Roya route just before the turning to Formigal.

Variant No.3. GR11 Góriz to Pineta via the Punta d'as Olas (Day 17). This is described in the text for Day 17.

Variant No.4. GR11.2 Circuit of the three *refugios* (Commencing Day 20). Two days required. Just past the Refugio de Viadós turn right, S then SE, beside the Barranco de la Ribereta to the Collado de Eriste or Collado de Forqueta, 2860m. Go down E to the Refugio d'Angel Orus or Refugio d'el Forcau, 2095m. The next day go N then E to the Collada de la Pllana, 2702m. Go down E to the Ibón Pequeño de Batisielles, 1960m. From here go E across a little pass, then NNE and some time later NW, down to the Refugio d'Estós, 1890m.

Variant No.5. GR11 Collado de Vallibierna to Refugio de Llausét (Day 22). Go down SE from the pass to the junction at 2410m. Turn right, S, and then pass along the northern shore of Ibón de Llausét, 2200m. Turn S then SE to the Refugio de Llausét, 1940m.

Variant No.6. GR11 Access from the small village of Aneto to Refugio de Llausét (Access to Day 22). Leave the village by the road going SW. A steep short-cut across a loop in the road leads to a trail, E, around the south ridge of Pic del Home and above the road. This joins the road eventually for a further 1km. Then a track is taken around the head of the valley to reach the Refugio de Llausét to the E.

Variant No.7. GR11 Refugio de Llausét to Refugio d'Anglós (part of the access from Aneto to the main route) (Access to Day 22). Go NW to the Ibón de Llausét passing N along its E side. Turn right, at a small tunnel mouth, to climb NNE to the Collado d'Anglós, 2429m. Go down E then NE to join with the main route just before the Refugio d'Anglós, 2220m. **Note:** It may be possible to climb the *pista* above the *refugio* and use the tunnels to the reservoir.

Variant No.8. GR11 Refugio de la Restanca to Refugio de Colomers via Pont de Rius (Day 24). The main route in this guide is designated GR11.18. Cross the dam and go down the wide track, N, to the Pont de Rius, 1700m. Take the *pista* NE for just under 3km, where a right branch is taken which climbs SE to the lake Basa de Montcasau, 1940m. Continue by a path to the Port de la Ribereta, 2350m. After some descent go over another smaller pass, 2238m, and then down, S, to join with the main route just W of the Refugio de Colomers, 2115m.

Variant No.9. GR11.20 Pont de Suert to Espot via Boi, Refugio de Colomina, Collado de Saburo and Refugio Josep Maria Blanc (Access to Day 26). Three days are required. There is a road that gives access to Boi and Taull, but the GR11 takes a twisting route above the road and some 1–3km to the E. It goes in a NE direction with a long detour to the W around Serrahis, 1585m. It continues NE to Boi and then E to Taull to complete the first day. There is accommodation at Boi. Some 3km of road SE from Taull lead to a path continuing SE to Port de Rus, 2627m. Go down zigzags, E, to the Barranc de Rus, following the valley down ENE. Go up the valley opposite to climb to the Collada de Font Sobirana, 2425m. From there continue generally NE and over another small pass to reach the Refugio de Colomina, 2396m, and the end of the second day. Continue NE to the Collado de Saburó, 2670m, then down NE past the Refugio J.M. Blanc, 2364m. Follow the delightful Peguera valley down to Espot, 1320m.

Variant No.10. GR11.10 Les Escaldes to Cabana dels Esparvers via Refugio Cap del Rec (Day 33). Two days are required. The GR7 is taken SE from Les Escaldes, which lies a few kilometres S from Encamp down the main road. In about 50mins take the right branch, which climbs SSE to the Port de Perafita, 2570m. Pass into Spain and continue down SE and then generally ESE to reach the Refugio Cap del Rec, 1980m. Go E then SSE to Viliella before turning N beside the Riu de la Llosa to Cabana dels Esparvers, 2068m.

Variant No.11. GR11.8 Dórria to Planoles via Fornells de la Muntanya (Day 36). Follow the road S then W from Dórria to join with the main road below. Turn right, W then S, for 3mins before taking the turning SE then WSW to Fornells de la Muntanya, 1284m. Take the *pista* going E, to the S of the railway track. Cross to the N side some time later to enter Planés, 1180m, and the main route of the GR11. Continue to Planoles, 1137m.

Variant No.12. GR11.7 Núria to Collado de la Marrana via Refugio Coma de Vaca (Day 38). This starts around the eastern side of the Estany de Núria, gradually climbing to 2100m where it contours into the Freser valley. It eventually drops down to the Refugio Coma de Vaca and continues up the upper Freser valley to the Collado de Marrana and the GR11. In bad weather this is a good alternative to the higher route.

APPENDIX 1
Glossary

(A) = Aragón (B) = Basque (C) = Catalan

Abri	Cabin	Canal	Canal, narrow valley
Achar (A)	Narrow pass		
Agua	Water	Cap (C)	Small hill
Aguja	Needle	Capella	Chapel
Alt	High	Carrer (C)	Street
Alto	High	Carretera	Road
Arroyo	Stream	Casa	House
Avenida	Avenue	Cascada	Waterfall
Avinguda (C)	Avenue	Caserio	Farm
Azul	Blue	Castillo	Castle
		Circo	Coombe
Baix	Low	Clot	Wide valley
Balle (A)	Valley	Col	Pass
Balneario	Thermal baths	Cola	Tail
Baxo	Low	Coll (C)	Pass
Biskar (B)	Shoulder	Colladeta	Small pass
Borda	Farm	Collado	Pass
Bosc (C)	Wood	Coma (A)	Coombe
Bosque	Wood	Creu (C)	Cross
Brecha	Gap	Cuello (A)	Pass
Caballo	Horse	Dalt	High
Cabana	Cabin		
Cabezo	Small hill	Embalse	Artificial lake
Cabo	Cape	Entibo (A)	Artificial lake
Cala (C)	Small bay	Ermita	Hermitage
Calle	Street	Espelunga (A)	Cave
Calm (C)	Bare plateau	Estacion	Station
Camino	Clear track	Estazion (A)	Station
Campo	Meadow area	Estiba (A)	Summer pasture above the woods
Can (C)	House		

Fabrica	Factory	Obago (C)	Dark
Faja	Ledge	Orri	Stone shelter or hut
Faro	Lighthouse	Paso	Pass
Faxa (A)	Ledge	Paul	Boggy area
Feixa (C)	Ledge	Pena (A)	Crag
Font (C)	Spring	Pic (C)	Peak
Fronton (B)	Pelota wall	Pica (C)	Peak
Fuén (A)	Spring	Pico	Peak
Fuente	Spring	Pla (C)	Flat area
		Placa	Town square
Gaina (B)	Summit	Plan (A)	Flat area
Glera (A)	Scree slope	Pont (A,C)	Bridge
Gran	Large or great	Port (C)	Pass
		Portella	Small pass
Hospital	Inn (in the	Prado	Meadow
	mountains)	Presa	Dam
Hostal	Hostel (small hotel)	Puen (A)	Bridge
		Puente	Bridge
Ibon (A)	Glacial lake	Puerto	Pass
Iturri (B)	Spring	Pui	Peak
		Puig (C)	Peak
Jussa (C)	Low		
		Rec (C)	Narrow valley
		Refugi (C)	Mountain hut
Lac (A)	Lake	Refugio	Mountain hut
Lago	Lake	Regata	Stream
Limpias	Clean	Rio	River
Llano	Flat area	Riu (C)	River
		Rivereta	Stream
Mas (C)	House		
Mendi	Mountain	San	Saint
Merendero	Picnic area	Sant (C)	Saint
Mig	Middle	Santa	Saint
Moli (C)	Mill	Santuario	Sanctuary
Monasterio	Monastery	Selba (A)	Wood
Monte	Mountain	Serra (C)	Mountain range
Muga (A,B)	Frontier marker	Sobira (C)	High, upper
		Soum	Rounded mountain
Negre	Black		top
Nord	North		

Sud	South	Tuc (C)	Sharp summit
		Tuca (A,C)	Sharp summit
Torrente	Mountain stream		
Tossal (C)	Hill	Val (A)	Valley
Tozal (A)	Steep hill, promontory	Vall (C)	Valley
		Valle	Valley

APPENDIX 2
Bibliography

Classic Walks in the Pyrenees – Kev Reynolds – The Oxford Illustrated Press

GR11 Senderos de Gran Recorrido – Various – Prames S.A.

GR11 Senda Pirenaica, mapas de etapa 1:40,000 – Prames S.A. (Recommended for maps)

GR11 Senders de Gran Recorregut No.1 – Various – Publicaciones del'Abadia de Montserrat S.A.

GR11 Senders de Gran Recorregut No.2 – Various

Pyrenees High Level Route – Georges Veron – Gastons-West Col Publications

La Senda, Grande Traversee des Pyrénées Espagnoles par le GR11 – Jean François Rodriguez – Rando Editions

Senda Pyrenaica, Topoguia del Sendero Aragones – Various – FAM

The Pyrenees, The Rough Guide – Marc Dubin – Rough Guides

Trekking the Pyrenees – Douglas Streatfeild-James – Trailblazer Publications

Walks and Climbs in the Pyrenees – Kev Reynolds – Cicerone Press

APPENDIX 3
Route Summary

Day and Stage	Height gain (m)	loss (m)	Time	Dist. (km)	Acc. Dist. (km)
1 Cabo Higuer – Vera de Bidasoa	830	815	7hrs 15mins	30	30
2 Vera Bidasoa – Elizondo	1130	985	7hrs 15mins	30	60
3 Elizondo – Puerto de Urkiaga	1050	340	5hrs 35mins	18.5	78.5
4 Puerto de Urkiaga – Burguete	680	695	5hrs	16	94.5
5 Burguete – Fábrica de Orbaiceta	600	660	5hrs	20.5	115
6 Fábrica de Orbaiceta – Casas de Irati	400	380	4hrs 15mins	16.5	131.5
7 Casas de Irati – Ochagavia	670	760	4hrs 20mins	14.5	146
8 Ochagavia – Isaba	710	660	5hrs 35mins	23.8	169.8
9 Isaba – Zuriza	1300	890	6hrs 30mins	18.5	188.3
10 Zuriza – La Mina	735	740	4hrs 05mins	12	200.3
11 La Mina – Candanchù	990	670	6hrs	22	222.3
12 Candanchù – Sallent de Gállego	880	1125	6hrs 10mins	22.3	244.6
13 Sallent de Gállego – Refugio de Respomuso	925	30	3hrs 45mins	11.8	256.4
14 Refugio de Respomuso – Balneario de Panticosa	690	1250	5hrs 25mins	13.3	269.7
15 Balneario de Panticosa – San Nicholás de Bujaruelo	940	1240	6hrs 50mins	20.5	290.2

Day Stage	Height gain (m)	loss (m)	Time	Dist. (km)	Acc. Dist. (km)
16 San Nicholás de Bujaruelo – Ref. de Góriz	1180	360	6hrs	22.5	312.7
17 Ref. de Góriz – Circo de Pineta	880	1750	7hrs 10mins	13.5	326.2
17 variant Ref. de Góriz – Circo de Pineta	590	1460	6hrs 40mins	11.5	
18 Circo de Pineta – Parzán	880	1025	5hrs 25mins	18	344.2
19 Parzán – Viadós	1445	850	6hrs	19.5	363.7
20 Viadós – Ref. d'Estós	860	710	4hrs 15mins	11.5	375.2
21 Estós – Ref. del Puente de Coronas	740	650	5hrs 10mins	18.5	393.7
22 Puente de Coronas – Hospital de Viella	1070	1420	7hrs 45mins	19.5	413.2
23 Hospital de Viella – Ref. de la Restanca	770	390	4hrs 10mins	10.5	423.7
24 Ref. de la Restanca – Ref. de Colomers	660	555	3hrs 40mins	7.5	431.2
25 Ref. de Colomers – Espot	500	1295	6hrs	19.5	450.7
26 Espot – La Guingueta	175	550	2hrs 30mins	9.5	460.2
27 La Guingueta – Bordas de Nibrós	1565	1030	6hrs 50mins	14.5	474.7
28 Bordas de Nibrós – Tavascan	400	760	3hrs 20mins	8.5	483.2
29 Tavascan – Àreu	1120	1015	6hrs 20mins	17.5	500.7
30 Àreu – Ref. de Baiau (J.M. Montfort)	1350	60	5hrs 30mins	15.5	516.2
31 Ref. de Baiau – Arans	750	1905	6hrs 10mins	15	531.2
32 Arans – Encamp	1010	1090	4hrs 45mins	14.5	545.7

Day Stage	Height gain (m)	loss (m)	Time	Dist. (km)	Acc. Dist. (km)
33 Encamp – Cabana dels Esparvers	1350	560	6hrs	20.5	566.2
34 C. dels Esparvers – Ref. de Malniu	810	740	4hrs	10.3	576.5
35 Ref. de Malniu – Puigcerdà	95	1030	3hrs 20mins	15	591.5
36 Puigcerdà – Planoles	1020	1085	7hrs	26.5	618
37 Planoles – Núria	1600	770	6hrs 30mins	21	639
38 Núria – Setcases	1080	1780	6hrs 20mins	21	660
39 Setcases – Beget	820	1575	6hrs 30mins	22	682
40 Beget – Sant Aniol d'Aguja	690	740	4hrs 40mins	16.5	698.5
41 Sant Aniol d'Aguja – Albanyà	685	910	6hrs 15mins	18	716.5
42 Albanyà – La Vajol	860	550	6hrs 55mins	27	743.5
43 La Vajol – Requesens	830	880	6hrs 20mins	24.5	768
44 Requesens – Sant Quirze de Colera	575	910	6hrs 15mins	26	794
45 Sant Quirze de Colera – El Port de la Selva	775	925	6hrs 40mins	27	821
46 El Port de la Selva – Cabo de Creus	445	440	4hrs 20mins	16	837

Totals

Total distance	837km
Total ascent	39520m
Total descent	39520m
Total time	256hrs

NOTES

NOTES

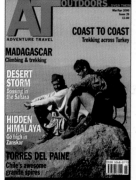

LISTING OF CICERONE GUIDES

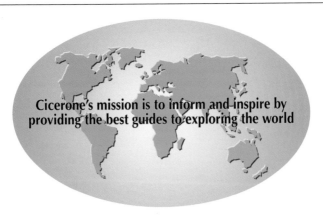

Cicerone's mission is to inform and inspire by
providing the best guides to exploring the world

Since its foundation over 30 years ago, Cicerone has specialised in publishing guidebooks and has built a reputation for quality and reliability. It now publishes nearly 300 guides to the major destinations for outdoor enthusiasts, including Europe, UK and the rest of the world.

Written by leading and committed specialists, Cicerone guides are recognised as the most authoritative. They are full of information, maps and illustrations so that the user can plan and complete a successful and safe trip or expedition – be it a long face climb, a walk over Lakeland fells, an alpine traverse, a Himalayan trek or a ramble in the countryside.

With a thorough introduction to assist planning, clear diagrams, maps and colour photographs to illustrate the terrain and route, and accurate and detailed text, Cicerone guides are designed for ease of use and access to the information.

If the facts on the ground change, or there is any aspect of a guide that you think we can improve, we are always delighted to hear from you.

Cicerone Press
2 Police Square Milnthorpe Cumbria LA7 7PY
Tel:01539 562 069   Fax:01539 563 417
e-mail:info@cicerone.co.uk   web:www.cicerone.co.uk

CICERONE